*CRITICAL ANTHOLOGIES OF NONFICTION WRITING*™

# CRITICAL PERSPECTIVES ON THE GREAT DEPRESSION

*Edited by*
*PAUL KUPPERBERG*

THE ROSEN PUBLISHING GROUP, INC.
NEW YORK

*To my dad, who lived this story*

Published in 2005 by The Rosen Publishing Group, Inc.
29 East 21st Street, New York, NY 10010

First Edition

**Library of Congress Cataloging-in-Publication Data**
Critical perspectives on the Great Depression / edited by Paul Kupperberg.—1st ed.
      p. cm.—(Critical anthologies of nonfiction writing)
Includes bibliographical references and index.
ISBN 1-4042-0061-4 (library binding)
1. United States—History—1933–1945—Sources—Juvenile literature. 2. United States—History—1919–1933—Sources—Juvenile literature. 3. New Deal, 1933–1939—Sources—Juvenile literature. 4. Depressions—1929—United States—Sources—Juvenile literature. I. Kupperberg, Paul. II. Series.
E806.C74 2005
973.917—dc22

2004000185

*Manufactured in the United States of America*

**On the cover:** A 1937 Russell Lee photograph of a North Dakota farm family.

# CONTENTS

# INTRODUCTION

‸ he only thing we have to fear is fear itself.

—President Franklin D. Roosevelt,
first inaugural address, March 4, 1933

Social Security. The federal income tax. Unemployment insurance. Welfare. The Federal Deposit Insurance Corporation (FDIC). The Tennessee Valley Authority (TVA). The National Labor Relations Board. The Securities and Exchange Commission (SEC). The Federal Housing Authority (FHA).

These are just some of the federal institutions and agencies that today many Americans either take for granted or resent for their high cost and intrusion into their lives and businesses. Before October 29, 1929—the day of the worst stock market crash in U.S. history and the unofficial start of the Great Depression—the creation of these and dozens of other federal institutions designed to help struggling Americans and protect their earnings would have been unthinkable to the citizens of the United States.

Americans of the early twentieth century had become accustomed to a laissez-faire (hands-off) style of government in which big business was allowed to generate wealth with little or no oversight from the government and little regard for the security of its workers or investors. Following the stock market crash and the nation's descent into a decadelong depression, however, these new federal programs helped pull the United States out of the depths of the greatest economic disaster ever to strike the country.

Very few people saw the crash and Depression coming. Ever since 1919 and the end of World War I (1914–1917), the United States had been on what appeared to be an ever-rising tide of economic growth with no end in sight. Veterans coming home from a horrific war returned to family members who had sacrificed luxuries and pleasures for the war effort. Buoyed by the United States' newfound global influence and strength, and flush with victory after years of adversity, Americans were in the mood to cut loose and celebrate. This period became known as the Roaring Twenties and the swinging Jazz Age, a decade of exuberance, excess, and wild abandon. While the Eighteenth Amendment had ushered in Prohibition by out-lawing the transportation and sale of alcoholic beverages in 1919, anyone wanting a drink knew where to find the nearest speakeasy (an illegal bar) for a shot of banned whiskey. The illegal alcohol was often accompanied by the hot sounds of a popular new form of music largely pioneered by African Americans—jazz.

The nation was fairly exploding with prosperity, innova-tion, and creativity. With only a little money down and little government regulation or interference, anyone could invest in the booming stock market and find themselves—on paper, at least—instantly wealthy. Air travel went from being a novelty craze to a commercial enterprise following Charles Lindbergh's successful 1927 solo flight across the Atlantic Ocean. At the same time, Americans bought millions of Henry Ford's new

Model A automobiles, helping to create the most mobile society in the history of the world. F. Scott Fitzgerald, Theodore Dreiser, and Ernest Hemingway brought literature into the modern and more cynical age with such works as *The Great Gatsby*, *An American Tragedy*, and *A Farewell to Arms*—books that featured flawed heroes, a loss of idealism, and sharp social critiques—while motion pictures learned to talk, starting with *The Jazz Singer* in 1927.

The United States of the 1920s seemed unstoppable. "The chief business of the American people is business," President Calvin Coolidge told the press in 1925, and no one could argue with that assessment. For most of its first century as an independent nation, the United States had been a largely agrarian society. By the end of the first third of the twentieth century, however, the country had become far more urban and industrialized. For the first time in the nation's history, a majority of Americans lived in cities rather than on farms. The nation was growing and booming, but the federal government remained small, staying out of the way of big business. It operated with a bureaucracy that can only be called minuscule compared to today's hundreds of thousands of federal workers who keep the monolithic machine of government humming.

Between May 1928 and September 1929, the average price of stocks (shares, or portions, of ownership of a company) rose 40 percent, while the volume of daily stock sales rose from 2 to 3 million shares per day to more than 5 million. As stock prices continued to soar, investors kept jumping on board the moneymaking wagon. All of this purchasing activity inflated the price of stocks well beyond their actual value.

Eventually, market forces would bring the stock prices down to a more reasonable level, one that reflected the actual health of the companies whose shares investors were madly snatching up.

On Tuesday, October 29, 1929, that's exactly what happened. Stocks plummeted, quickly plunging the United States and the rest of the world into the throes of the Great Depression. In a single day, billions of dollars were lost. It is estimated that on the New York Stock Exchange alone, losses exceeded $8 billion—this at a time when the average per capita urban household income was $750 per year and $273 for farming households. More than 16 million shares were frantically traded in a futile attempt to stanch the financial bloodletting. Small investors, who would have realized a large profit if they had sold their stock the day before, were suddenly forced to sell in order to avoid watching the value of their stocks sink even lower. Many lost everything they had on a day so catastrophic and bleak that it became known simply as Black Tuesday.

Jazz Age exuberance and excess turned almost immediately into desperation and deprivation. Banks and businesses failed, the money supply shrank, and by 1932, the unemployment rate would reach a staggering 23.6 percent (eventually peaking during the Depression at 24.9 percent), as more than 13 million Americans lost their jobs. Relief efforts were organized across the country, and families with no source of income were forced to stand in the infamous breadlines and eat at soup kitchens set up by churches and charities. These charitable public institutions provided the only reliable source of food for many Americans.

Hundreds of thousands of the unemployed took to the road, seeking work at any wage in any locality. Entire families began a westward migration to the rich agricultural valleys of California from the states of Kansas, Oklahoma, Texas, New Mexico, Nevada, and Arkansas. These farming and ranching states were suffering the added tragedy of one of the worst droughts in history, which turned a large section of the nation into what became known as the Dust Bowl.

President Herbert Hoover took a number of steps to stem the rising tide of desperation, spur the economy, and protect Americans' savings. But it was not until newly elected President Franklin D. Roosevelt took office in 1933 that the federal government's response to the Depression was equal to the magnitude of the crisis. As the Democratic nominee for president, Roosevelt had promised, "I pledge you, I pledge myself, to a new deal for the American people."

Roosevelt was as good as his word. In the first 100 days of his administration, his promised New Deal instituted an extensive program of legislative activity, sending recovery bill after recovery bill to a Congress that, unsure how to respond, had not done nearly enough to help the American people through this unprecedented financial catastrophe. Under the president's guidance, Congress created, in swift succession, the Agricultural Adjustment Administration (AAA), the Civilian Conservation Corps (CCC), the Farm Credit Administration (FCA), the Federal Deposit Insurance Corporation (FDIC), the Federal Emergency Relief Administration (FERA), the National Recovery Act (NRA), the Public Works Administration (PWA), and the Tennessee Valley Authority (TVA), to name just a few of the dozens of New Deal programs that were eventually set up. These federal agencies—along with a rash of banking, securities, and credit acts that followed—were all aimed at getting Americans back to work and the floundering economy back on track.

But for all the efforts of FDR (as Roosevelt would often be referred to) and his dedicated administration, it would be more than a decade before the nation and the world would truly recover from the economic downward spiral begun on Black Tuesday.

# CHAPTER ONE

# PEOPLE, PLACES, AND ENVIRONMENTS: SORROW AND SUFFERING DURING THE DEPRESSION

**"Stocks Collapse in 16,410,030-Share Day, but Rally at Close Cheers Brokers; Bankers Optimistic, to Continue Aid"**
*From the* New York Times
*October 30, 1929*

*It is difficult to point to any single cause of the stock market crash of 1929, but an editorial in the* New York Times *just days before the calamitous events of October 29 warned against the "orgy of speculation" that was driving stock prices unreasonably high. (Speculation is the purchasing of cheap stocks in the hopes of making a profit by selling when their prices rise.) In an earlier article published on March 24, 1929, a* New York Times *reporter claimed: "Playing the stock market has become a major American pastime. It is quite true that the people who know the least about the stock market have made the most money out of it in the last few months. Fools who rushed in where wise men feared to tread ran up high gains."*

*Fools continued rushing in until October 29, 1929, when, following two troubled days in which the stock market lost nearly one-quarter of its value, the bottom finally fell out and stock prices crashed back to earth. By the time the plunge had been slowed and stock prices stabilized, the Dow Jones Industrial Average (which charts the performance of a group of popular stocks) had fallen 89 percent from its 1929 peak.*

———□———

Stock prices virtually collapsed yesterday, swept downward with gigantic losses in the most disastrous trading day in the stock market's history. Billions of dollars in open market values were wiped out as prices crumbled under the pressure of liquidation of securities which had to be sold at any price.

There was an impressive rally just at the close, which brought many leading stocks back from four to fourteen points from their lowest points of the day.

Trading on the New York Stock Exchange aggregated 16,410,030 shares; on the Curb, 7,096,300 shares were dealt in. Both totals far exceeded any previous day's dealings.

From every point of view, in the extent of losses sustained, in total turnover, in the number of speculators wiped out, the day was the most disastrous in Wall Street's history. Hysteria swept the country and stocks went overboard for just what they would bring at forced sale.

Efforts to estimate yesterday's market losses in dollars are futile because of the vast number of securities quoted over the counter and on out-of-town exchanges on which no calculations are possible. However, it was estimated that 880 issues, on the New York Stock Exchange, lost between $8,000,000,000 and $9,000,000,000 yesterday . . .

### *Change Is Expected Today*

That there will be a change today seemed likely from statements made last night by financial and business leaders.

Organized support will be accorded to the market from the start, it is believed, but those who are staking their all on the country's leading securities are placing a great deal of confidence, too, in the expectation that there will be an overnight change in sentiment; that the counsel of cool heads will prevail and that the mob psychology which has been so largely responsible for the market's debacle will be broken.

The fact that the leading stocks were able to rally in the final fifteen minutes of trading yesterday was considered a good omen, especially as the weakest period of the day had developed just prior to that time and the minimum prices for the day had then been established. It was a quick run-up which followed the announcement that the American Can directors had declared an extra dividend of $1. The advances in leading stocks in this last fifteen minutes represented a measurable snapback from the lows. American Can gained 10; United States Steel Common, 7 1/2, General Electric, 12; New York Central, 14 1/2, Anaconda Copper, 9 1/2; Chrysler Motors, 5 1/4; Montgomery Ward, 4 1/4 and Johns Manville, 8. Even with these recoveries the losses of these particular stocks, and practically all others, were staggering.

Yesterday's market crash was one which largely affected rich men, institutions, investment trusts and others who participate in the stock market on a broad and intelligent scale. It was not the margin traders who were caught in the rush to sell, but the rich men of the country who are able to swing blocks of 5,000, 10,000 up to 100,000 shares of high-priced stocks. They went overboard with no more consideration than the little trader who was swept out on the first day of the market's upheaval, whose prices, even at their lowest of last Thursday, now look high in comparison.

The market on the rampage is no respecter of persons. It washed fortune after fortune away yesterday and financially crippled thousands of individuals in all parts of the world. It was not until after the market had closed that the financial district began to realize that a good-sized rally had taken place and that there was a stopping place on the downgrade for good stocks.

### Third Day of Collapse

The market has now passed through three days of collapse, and so violent has it been that most authorities believe that the end is not far away. It started last Thursday, when 12,800,000 shares were dealt in on the Exchange, and holders of stocks commenced to learn just what a decline in the market means. This was followed by a moderate rally on Friday and entirely normal conditions on Saturday, with fluctuations on a comparatively narrow scale and with the efforts of the leading bankers to stabilize the market evidently successful. But the storm broke anew on Monday, with prices slaughtered in every direction, to be followed by yesterday's tremendous trading of 16,410,030 shares . . .

### Huge Blocks Offered at Opening

The opening bell on the Stock Exchange released such a flood of selling as has never before been witnessed in this country. The failure of the market to rally consistently on the previous day, the tremendous shrinkage of open market values and the wave of hysteria which appeared to sweep the country brought an avalanche of stock to the market to be sold at whatever price it would bring.

From the very first quotation until thirty minutes after 10 o'clock it was evident that the day's market would be an unprecedented one. In that first thirty-minutes of trading stocks were poured out in 5,000, 10,000, 20,000 and 50,000 share blocks at tremendous sacrifices as compared with the previous closing. The declines ranged from a point or so to as much as 29 1/2 points, and the reports of opening prices brought selling into the market in confused volume that has never before been equaled.

In this first half hour of trading on the Stock Exchange a total of 3,250,800 shares were dealt in. The volume of the first twenty-six blocks of stock dealt in at the opening totaled more than 630,000 shares.

There was simply no near-by demand for even the country's leading industrial and railroad shares, and many millions of dollars in values were lost in the first quotations tapped out. All considerations other than to get rid of the stock at any price were brushed aside.

### Brokerage Offices Crowded

Wall Street was a street of vanished hopes, of curiously silent apprehension and of a sort of paralyzed hypnosis yesterday. Men and women crowded the brokerage offices, even those who have been long since wiped out, and followed the figures on the tape. Little groups gathered here and there to discuss the fall in prices in hushed and awed tones. They were participating in the making of financial history. It was the consensus of bankers and brokers alike that no such scenes ever again will be witnessed by this generation. To most of those who have been in the market it is all the more awe-inspiring because their financial history is limited to bull markets.

The machinery of the New York Stock Exchange and the Curb market were unable to handle the tremendous volume of trading which went over them. Early in the day they kept up well, because most of the trading was in big blocks, but as the day progressed the tickers fell further and further behind, and as on the previous big days of this week and last it was only by printing late quotations of stocks on the bond tickers and by the ten-minute flashes on stock prices put out by Dow, Jones & Co. and the Wall Street News Bureau that the financial district could get any idea of what was happening in the wild mob of brokers on the Exchange and the Curb.

## From "Cows and Horses Are Hungry"
**By Meridel Le Sueur**
**From American Mercury**
**September 1934**

And then the dispossessed were drawn west—from Kansas, Oklahoma, Texas, New Mexico; from Nevada and Arkansas, families, tribes, dusted out, tractored out. Carloads, caravans, homeless and hungry; twenty thousand and fifty thousand and a hundred thousand and two hundred thousand. They streamed over the mountains, hungry and restless—restless as ants, scurrying to find work to do—to lift, to push, to pull, to pick, to cut—anything, any burden to bear, for food. The kids are hungry.

—*From* The Grapes of Wrath, *by John Steinbeck (1939)*

*Even as Americans struggled through the early—and worst—years of the Great Depression, the Plains states were struck by an added disaster. A severe drought had plagued the region since the early 1930s, worsening as farmers continued to squeeze what crops they could out of the depleted soil. Soon, the land was "farmed out." It was bone-dry from lack of rain, and as a result, its nutrient-rich topsoil had been blown away by the winds that blasted across the Plains. Meridel Le Sueur, a reporter and children's book author, recorded her impressions of this blighted landscape and its beleaguered people in an article for* American Mercury.

—□—

## I.

When you drive through the Middle West droughty country you try not to look at the thrusting out ribs of the horses and cows, but you get so you can't see anything else but ribs, like hundreds of thousands of little beached hulks. It looks like the bones are rising right up out of the skin. Pretty soon, quite gradually, you begin to know that the farmer, under his rags, shows his ribs, too, and the farmer's wife is as lean as his cows, and his children look tiny and hungry.

Drive through Elbow Lake, Otter Tail County, Elk River and Kandiyohi County, Big Stone County, Yellow Medicine County and Mille Lacs, and you'll see the same thing. These are only the counties that are officially designated as in the

droughty area by the Federal government. This is only in
Minnesota. In the Dakotas they say cattle are leaning up against
the fences. There is a shortage of water as well as of pasturage.

If you are officially in the droughty areas you will come in
on the government purchasing of starving cattle. On May 31, the
day after the last hot wind and the temperature at 112° in some
areas, the papers announced the working plan of the machinery
set up by the Federal government to aid farmers in the drought
stricken areas of the Northwest. The animals will be bought and
those that are not too far gone will be fattened and given to the
F.E.R.A. [Federal Emergency Relief Administration] for the relief
departments. If you're on the breadlines you'll be getting some
starved meat for your own starved bones. They could feed you
some choice farmer's ribs, too. But you can't buy up farmers and
their wives and shoot them. Not directly.

The government has been pushing straw into these communities all winter to keep the cattle from starving for lack of
grain until the pasturage came in. Well, now there is no pas-
ture. The grass is brown and burnt as if it might be mid-August
instead of May and June. The farmer is milked at one end and
given relief at another. Well, the farmer says, they wanted a
scarcity, and by God, now they have it. They shot off the pigs
and cows, they tried to keep what was left alive because they
couldn't feed them, now they're trying to keep them from dying
off and rotting on the ground and making too big a stench.

The farmer can't sell his cattle to the stockyards.
They're too far gone, too thin. The cattle thus turned over to the
government will be left temporarily on the farms, fed by the
administration and then moved to the packing houses or

redistributed to other farmers or turned directly over to relief channel . . .

## II.

The farmer has been depressed a long time. For the last three years he has been going over into the abyss of pauperism by the thousands. This spring after a terrible winter there was no rain. The village where I live has not exchanged money for two years. They have bartered and exchanged their produce. Last year some had nothing to exchange. We cut down trees in the front yard for fuel and tried to live off the miserable crop of potatoes of last year.

Since April there has been hope of rain and even up until the day after Decoration Day, until that bitter afternoon when the hot winds came and made any hope after that impossible. During April the farmers said that the winter wheat would be all right if it would rain even next week. The peas went in. They raise a lot of peas for the canneries both in Wisconsin and Minnesota. The peas came up a little ways and then fell down as if they had been mowed down. We waited to put in the corn day after day.

Then came a terrifying wind from the Dakotas, blew tens of thousands of dollars worth of onion seed away and half of North Dakota blew into Ohio with the spring sowing. That wind was a terror and blew dust and seed so high you couldn't drive through it in mid-day.

A kind of terror grew in the folk. It was too much, added up with the low prices they got, the drought, heat and high wind. A peculiar thing happened. Very much like what happened in the flu terror after the war. No one went outdoors. They all shut themselves up as if some terrific crisis, some horrible massacre, were about to occur. The last day of the wind, the radio announced every half hour that there was no menace in the dust, it would hurt no one actually. The wind died down, but it didn't rain. Well, they said, it will rain. It has to rain sometime. The winter wheat and rye began to whiten. A thin stand. You could sit in your house and look about and see the fields whiten and the wheat seemed to go back into the ground. You could see it stand still and then creep back into the ground.

But the farmers kept on ploughing in case it would rain. First you had to plough with two horses and then with four. You couldn't rip the earth open and when you did, a fume of dust went up like smoke, and a wind from hell whipped the seed out. Some planted their corn, though, in corn-planting time, some waited for rain. They waited until the day after Decoration Day.

Every day the pastures became worse. The grass became as dry as straw in May and the cattle lost their flesh quickly. They weren't too well padded because of scarce food all winter. You had to look for a green spot every morning. Children were kept out of school to herd the cattle around near streams and creeks. Some farmers cut down trees so the cattle could eat the leaves even if they were poor picking. The leaves on the trees are poor, falling off already in some places due to the searing, driving wind and the lack of moisture at their roots. The man up the road has turned his cows into his winter wheat which is thin as a young man's first beard anyway.

On Decoration Day the wind started again, blowing hot as a blast from hell and the young corn withered as if under machine gun fire, the trees in two hours looked as if they had been beaten. The day after Decoration Day it was so hot you couldn't sit around looking at the panting cattle and counting their ribs and listening to that low cry that is an awful asking. We got in the car and drove slowly through the sizzling countryside.

Not a soul was in sight. It was like a funeral. The houses were closed up tight, the blinds drawn, the windows and doors closed. There seemed to be a menace in the air made visible. It was frightening. You could hear the fields crack and dry, and the only movement in the down-driving heat was the dead writhing of the dry blighted leaves on the twigs. The young corn about four spears up was falling down like a fountain being slowly turned off.

There was something terrifying about this visible sign of disaster. It went into your nostrils so you couldn't breathe: the smell of hunger. It made you count your own ribs with terror. You don't starve in America. Everything looks good. There is something around the corner. Everyone has a chance. That's all over now. The whole country cracks and rumbles and cries out in its terrible leanness, stripped with exploitation and terror—and as sign and symbol, bones—bones showing naked and spiritless, showing decay and crisis and a terrific warning, bare and lean in Mid-America.

We kept driving very slowly, about as slowly as you go to a funeral, with no one behind us, meeting no one on the road. The corpse was the very earth. We kept looking at the body of the earth, at the bare and mortgaged and unpainted houses like hollow pupas when the life has gone. They looked stripped as if after a raid. As if a terrible army had just gone through. It used to be hard to look at the fat rich-seeming farms and realize that they were mortgaged to the hilt and losing ground every year, but not now. Now it stands a visible sign. You can see the marks of the ravagers. The mark of that fearful exploitation stands on the landscape visible, known, to be reckoned with.

The cows were the only thin flesh visible. They stood in the poor shade of the stripped and dying trees, breathing heavily, their great ribs showing like the ribs of decaying boats beached and deserted. But you knew that from behind all those drawn blinds hundreds of eyes were watching that afternoon, that no man, woman or child could sit down and read a book or lie down to any dreams. Through all these windows eyes were watching—watching the wheat go, the rye go, the corn, peas, potatoes go. Everywhere in those barricaded houses were eyes drawn back to the burning windows looking out at next winter's food slowly burning in the fields. You look out and see the very food of your next winter's sustenance visibly, physically dying beneath your eyes, projecting into you your future hungers.

The whole countryside that afternoon became terrifying, not only with its present famine but with the foreshadowing of its coming hunger. No vegetables now, and worst of all, no milk. The countryside became monstrous with this double doom. Every house is alike in suffering as in a flood, every cow, every field mounting into hundreds, into thousands, from State to State. You try not to look at the ribs, but pretty soon you are looking only at ribs.

Then an awful thing happened. The sun went down behind the ridge, dropped low, and men and women began to pour out of the houses, the children lean and fleet as rats, the tired lean farm women looking to see what had happened. The men ran into their fields, ran back for water and they began to water their lands with buckets and cups, running, pouring the puny drops of water on the baked earth as if every minute might count now. The children ran behind the cows urging them to eat the harsh dry grass. It looked like an evacuated countryside, with the people running out after the enemy had passed. Not a word was spoken. In intense silence they hurried down the rows with buckets and cups, watering the wilted corn plants, a gargantuan and terrible and hopeless labor. Some came out with horses and ploughs and began stirring up the deadly dust. If the field was a slope, barrels were filled, and a primitive irrigation started. Even the children ran with cups of water, all dogged silent, mad, without a word. A certain madness in it all, like things that are done after unimaginable violence.

We stop and talk to a farmer. His eyes are bloodshot. I can hardly see from the heat and the terrible emotion . . . How do you think my cows look? he asks. I think they are a little fatter today. I try not to look at his cows at all. Pretty thin, though, he says, pretty thin. I can see the fine jersey pelt beginning to sag and the bones rise out like sticks out of the sea at low tide.

We both know that a farmer across the river shot twenty-two of his cattle yesterday, and then shot himself. I look at him and I can see his clavicle and I know that his ribs are rising out of his skin, too. It is visible now, starvation and famine. So they are going to buy the starving cattle and shoot them and feed the rest to the breadlines. A man isn't worth anything— but a cow . . .

We drive on. When I shut my eyes the flesh burns the balls, and all I can see is ribs—the bones showing through.

## *"Pea-Pickers' Child Dies"*
## *By Lucrecia Penny*
### *From* **Survey Graphic**
### *July 1935*

But migrant families do not gather about soup kitchens, nor do they travel in boxcars or form impro- vised armies for protest demonstrations. They have, in fact, an extraordinary faculty for making themselves inconspicuous; they are the least noticeable of people and the most difficult to locate.

—*From* Ill Fares the Land: Migrants and Migratory Labor in the United States, *by Carey McWilliams (1941)*

*Cheap labor has long been a double-edged sword of the American economy. On the one hand, it enables products to be produced at a low cost. On the other hand, it creates a class of people who cannot afford to purchase what they help to produce. Among this nearly invisible underclass are migrant farmworkers who labor for a few dollars a day of backbreaking work.*

*It is difficult today to imagine the level of poverty and desperate, dangerous conditions facing the migrant workers of the Depression era. While the urban homeless found some small measure of assistance in the form of government relief programs, seasonal agricultural workers who lived on the road had no such institution to turn to for help. In this article, Lucrecia Penny observes the numbed sorrow and weary resignation of a migrant family left desolate by the death of one of the children.*

———□———

The death notice in the county paper was not more than two inches in depth but it had, nevertheless, its modest headline: PEA-PICKERS CHILD DIES. Already there had been three deaths in the pea-pickers' camp: a Mexican had been murdered, stabbed; a child had died of burns; a baby had died of what his young mother referred to as "a awful fever in his little stomach." And now the shallow headlines spoke of Zetilla Kane, the seventh child and only daughter of Joe and Jennie Bell Kane.

"We come from Texas," Joe Kane had told the "lady from the government." He sat on a box beside the makeshift stove that warmed the tent where Zetilla had died. The odor of onions stewed for a poultice still hovered in the air. Joe Kane's broad, blunt hands rested on his knees. His tall body slumped. His dark eyes showed a want of sleep.

"We been back three times in the five years we been messin' 'round like this without no home. They sure ain't nothin' in Texas for us. The last time we was back my woman even owned to that."

He glanced around the tent with its three cots for the family of nine—eight now—with its stove that once had been a gasoline container, with its oilcloth-covered table on which was a pan of boiled potatoes black with flies. He picked up a Western-story magazine from the pile of stove-wood at his feet, opened it and placed it over the potatoes.

"This here was sort of pushed on to me and Jennie Bell and the young ones. None of our folks—neither side—never lived like gypsies, and we sure never set out to. We ain't never owned nothin' much, but then we ain't had to move every time a crop was laid by neither, lessen we was a mind to. We always farmed it. Then back in 1930 things had got so dog-gone tough we sold off our furniture and radio and cow and chickens and all and pulled out of Texas for Missouri where my woman's folks is. We thought for sure we was goin' where things was better."

He paused and sat hunched over the little stove, gazing out across the camp-ground, playground of white and Mexican children, of dogs of a dozen breeds. A black and white puppy snapped at the heels of a goat leashed to a tent stake, and a little girl in a dirty chiffon dress from which torn ruffles fluttered like kite tails paused on a hopscotch field to drawl gently, "Cut it out, you durn fool dog."

"Zetilly like to had a spell over that there goat when we moved in. She was always after the boys to take her to 'see doat.' And they'd sure do it. They was sure silly over her. She'd had the whooping-cough back in Oregon and it got her flesh. She never tried to walk none after that; she'd just been learnin' when she took down."

He motioned across the camp-ground to where a Jesus Saves banner was pinned to a closed tent. "Them folks over there—that lame fellow they call Deacon and his wife—has went with Jennie Bell down to where Zetilly's at. You reckon we're goin' to have trouble with the County? Some say that they won't let you go to the buryin' or have a preacher at the funeral. It'd pretty near kill my woman. Back in Missouri they think preachin' can't start till about two benchfuls of her folks is there."

He sighed. "Our next to the last one was born in Missouri. That's him out there coughin' now. We thought we was goin' back to Missouri to get a place to farm it. Jennie Bell's folks had wrote and said they'd try to find us somethin'. Well, when we got there they was all on the County and there shore wasn't no sign of nothin' there for us. The County wanted to send us back to Texas but we couldn't see it that way, so we traded off our car for a Model T and twenty dollars to boot and pulled out for Kentucky. Before me and Jennie Bell was married I ust to work in coal mines and I didn't know but what I could get on again."

He shrugged his shoulders apologetically. "A body'll try any fool thing when he's up ag'in it. It never surprised me none though, when I seen I'd been stung some more. We sold our trailer then, and some old-time quilts that had been Jennie Bell's grandmammy's and wasn't thick enough to be much use to us noway, and we started on down toworge Texas. We got in a little cotton pickin' but cotton was sorry and we seen there wasn't no chance to make a trade for a place to stay another year, and we heard pickin' was good over in Arizona. Well, we went and it wasn't but we got in enough to keep us eatin' off and on, and we run into a fellow that said fruit pickin' was good out here, so we come on to California. We been messin' along like that ever since, pickin' hops and cotton and oranges and peas, prunin' a little and spacin' peaches and cuttin' lettuce and workin' at one crop and another, and then movie' on some more. We might's well be gypsies and be done with it. When Zetilly was born we was campin' on a picnic-ground up in Washington. We'd been up to see could we get on a homestead."

His voice shook and, waiting to gain control of it, he bent to straighten the stove-wood at his feet. "Zetilly was born on the road and she died on the road. The undertaker's is the first house she's ever been in, and some say the County don't aim for us to be there when she's buried. She sure did hate being left by herself. She was such a little thing and she wouldn't hardly rest a minute lessen some of us had holt of her. Do you reckon it's so that they don't aim for us to be there?"

It wasn't.

Joe and Jennie Bell Kane and their six sons went to the brief service at the undertaker's, followed Zetilla's body to the small grave the County had prepared for it. Deacon, his wife and five other pea-pickers went also. Deacon was short and white-haired and walked with a limp. It was he who selected the burial song from a book he carried in his pocket.

The minister from the local church said a prayer and spoke briefly to the little group at the undertaker's. He had to leave them and Deacon led the song at the grave. The local minister had spoken of immortality and reunion and incorruption, had dwelt upon the glory that is celestial. To his hearers his words were words without associations. It was different with the song that Deacon and the others sang, the song that told about "that beautiful city my Lord has prepared for His own."

They sang it vigorously, boldly, swinging eagerly from the final word of one verse to the beginning of another. It was at once a boast and a taunt hurled at those who might dare to disbelieve.

It had to be true. Hope of something better just ahead, in another state, in another season, had failed so often, but this time it could not fail. The beautiful city was real. It had to be. How else could they bear to leave Zetilla in the grave the County had dug for her—Zetilla, the frail, dark eyed baby who had liked to be held, who had died just as she was beginning to learn to sound the names of her six brothers?

There was nothing difficult to understand in the words of the song. The youngest of the Kane boys, the one with the cough, need not find them difficult to understand. There was no mention now of the exchange of terrestrial for celestial glory, of the putting off of the corruptible for the incorruptible. Simply, baldly, the song set forth the promise that what had made earthly life so sore a trial need not be feared in that beautiful city to which Zetilla had gone, that there one might have the necessities of life.

Vigorously, boldly, with an eager swing from verse to verse:

*"We'll never pay rent for our mansion,*
*The taxes will never come due;*

*Our garments will never grow threadbare,*
*But always be faceless and new."*

One of Joe Kane's broad, blunt hands held the hand of his
youngest son. The other rested awkwardly on his wife's shoulder, toyed with the collar of the pink rayon dress she wore. The
rayon, a deeper shade of pink then, had been new when they left
Texas. "But always be faceless and new." Boldly the song that
Deacon led offered the comfort of its promise to Zetilla's mother.

Perhaps already her baby was attired in faceless clothing and new, in a dress that was starched and ironed, in such
a dress as she might have worn to church on Children's Day
back in Missouri. Would there be tatting on the collar perhaps, a little yellow duck appliqued on the pocket? Zetilla's
mother hid her face with her hands and sobbed.

*"We'll never be hungry nor thirsty,*
*Nor languish in poverty there."*

Joe Kane's hand tightened its hold on the hand of the
child who had so recently been "next to the least one" and
was the least one now. The child coughed.

*"There'll never be crepe on the door-knob,*
*No funeral train in the sky;*
*No graves on the hillsides of glory,*
*For there we shall nevermore die."*

Jennie Bell Kane uncovered her face and pushed back
a brittle strand of blonde hair that was streaked with grey.
She was thirty-four. Whenever she told her age to the

women in the camps they shook their heads and made lamenting sounds. "These hard times sure ain't made none of us no younger," she sometimes said in apology.

"The old will be young there forever," they sang.

A woman had brought a tight bunch of wild flowers—lupin and California poppies and baby-blue-eyes—wrapped in a newspaper for Zetilla's grave. Zetilla's mother stooped when the song was ended and took four of the blossoms. She looked at her husband. Then she put her flowers back with the others, on the mound of earth beside the grave.

"I might's well leave 'em," she said brokenly. "I wouldn't have no place to press 'em. Back home we ust to press 'em in the Bible."

## "Trampling Out the Vintage"
### By Charles L. Todd
### From Common Sense
### July 1939

*By the mid-1930s, it was obvious that a federal program was needed to aid poor farmers and sharecroppers (poor farmers who planted on rented land and gave landlords a share of their profits or crops) who were burdened by poor harvests and low prices. The Resettlement Administration (RA), created in 1935, was the answer to this problem. The RA granted low-cost loans and assistance to struggling farmers. It also directed and funded the construction of regional resettlement camps for migrant farmworkers, the recultivation of land eroded by the Dust Bowl and poor*

*farming practices, and the establishment of controls for*
*river pollution and flood protection. The RA also had an*
*Information Division that helped promote the administration's*
*vital work by photographing the living conditions in these*
*rural areas and documenting the improvements wrought by*
*the RA. In 1937, the RA was incorporated into the U.S.*
*Department of Agriculture. Its name was changed to the*
*Farm Security Administration (FSA).*

*Charles L. Todd, an ethnographer and folk musicolo-*
*gist, documented the work of the FSA in California. In this*
*article written for* Common Sense, *Todd reports on the cre-*
*ation of FSA migratory labor camps in California's*
*Imperial Valley, sharp community opposition to them, and*
*the fragile hope for a spirit of compassion and friendship*
*to prevail.*

———□———

Imperial Valley has changed its tune. The richest agricultural
center in California and headquarters of the State's frontline
reactionary defense, Imperial has taken one New Deal agency
to its bosom. The Migratory Labor Camps, set up under the
Farm Security Administration in 1937, have won a real victory
over the forces of stupidity and wrath that made the Valley a
sink-hole of farm labor exploitation since the days of the first
irrigating ditch.

It wasn't an easy victory. The camps were bitterly
fought and hated from the beginning; the wonder is that a
single tent survived. Ask those men and women who pioneered at Brawley, Indio and Calipatria, and you'll find that
most of them prefer not to discuss it. John Steinbeck got the

story, but what he personally went through is known only to a few men who took him through it—men like Collins and Starkie. Those heroic families out of Oklahoma and Arkansas know the story too, but they have their fingers crossed, and they aren't talking. No, one must go to the opposition itself to hear what is happening in Imperial Valley: to the local service clubs, the Parent-Teachers Associations, the Chambers of Commerce, the lords of the local press, the Associated Farmers and the ordinary men and women who shouted themselves hoarse over the threat to their Americanism, their liberties, and their virtue.

There are some eleven Migratory Labor Camps scattered through California, and their stories are pretty much the same. In the little town of Brawley, for example, over three hundred dust-bowl families were huddled together in a dry riverbed a few miles out of town. The intimate details of their existence may be found in a dozen Farm Security Administration reports, in the files of the Simon J. Lubin society, in Steinbeck's *Grapes of Wrath*; or they may be studied personally in the Bakersfield area where the clean-up is by no means finished. Despite the unbelievable misery in that riverbed, the good citizens of Imperial Valley did nothing. A few half-humorously suggested that the "Okies" be lined up and shot; others sent half-hearted protests to the Health Department.

Then, one day in 1937, representatives of the Farm Security Administration, led by Tom Collins, walked into Brawley. Concluding an agreement for the purchase of a small plot of land at the edge of the town, they drew up plans for tent platforms, an office building, a nursery and a medical unit, three sanitary units with showerbaths and toilets, a tool-shed, a garage—in fact, all that goes into the making of a rough but livable community. Beyond lay the great orchards and vegetable acres where migrant labor was needed. Around them lived the big growers, the farm-factory-bank owners who in 1934 had banded themselves together as the Associated Farmer organization to "promote the prompt, orderly and efficient administration of justice." And over in the riverbed were 300 American families who had a very intimate knowledge of such "justice."

As plans for the government camp were being aired, the first to get upset was the editor of *The Brawley News*. The whole thing came straight out of Russia—no doubt about it! Next day an editorial informed the citizens of Brawley that the hammer and sickle would soon be hoisted on the very rim of town. The editor wasn't being funny either. He believed it. Asked how he feels about it now that the camp has been a reality for nearly two years, the editor is strangely quiet. Perhaps he is thinking of the day Tom Collins walked in and asked him how many red stripes there are in the American flag. He got caught on that one, so now he is a little suspicious of strangers. "Well, the damn camp is here now, and there's nothing we can do about it!" is the most one can get out of him. But there haven't been any more editorials on the subject and his reporters no longer check the hospital every day for new cases of typhoid and dysentery.

Next to cry havoc were the rental associations and more particularly the proprietress of an adjacent "tourist camp." "Business ruined!" . . . "Get up a petition!" . . .

"Send telegrams!" But it turned out, the "Okies" in the riverbed couldn't afford a dollar a day anyway. The rental associations soon got over it. Furthermore, with the riverbed cleaned out and the Okies scrubbing themselves under showerbaths every day, Brawley became a better place to live in. Tourists began to drop in. Today the tourist camp is prospering. Of course patriots are still muttering to themselves about "communism," but there haven't been any more petitions.

### "Hobo Brats"

One day, while men were still working on the tent platforms, a delegation of irate Parent-Teachers arrived at the camp. The question the ladies put was: "Are you going to make it possible for more of these hobo brats to go to school with our children?" More telegrams, more oratory in the Brawley school house. But a few weeks later a group of determined and well-scrubbed little Okies marched into the schools to start business learning the three R's. Statistics show that these children are "retarded" to a certain extent, but at least they now get as much milk as the others and the local Fauntleroys aren't quite so ready to call them dirty names. It might be added that a P.T.A. mother walked into camp recently to inspect the "Well Baby Clinic." Brawley mothers are now enthusiastic about their new day nursery—set up according to instructions from a government-paid nurse at the Migratory Labor Camp.

Meanwhile, up in the Indio Camp, young Wilbur Washburn, of Illinois, ascended the platform at the Coachella Valley High School and won first prize with an oration called

"Democracy versus Dictatorship." Among other things, this migrant child said: "We who have luxuries that only the wealthy families have under a dictatorship, have no idea of the terrors and crises caused solely by a dictator."

The school superintendent of Brawley has not yet been appeased. "These camps," he says, "are another example of the evils of a paternalistic government. The students who come in here from the camp are getting accustomed to clinging to the government's skirts. What will become of their initiative? Kids must learn to fight their way to the top. I did it myself. Every good American has done it!" The superintendent never went down to the riverbed. He is a good Republican. But he's mighty glad that the schools aren't being closed periodically because of typhoid, and he's not getting up any more petitions.

And what of the Associated Farmers? Mr. Hugh Osborne, Imperial County Supervisor and author of the famous phrase, "We know a better way!" speaks:

"The whole proposition is Communist through and through! It stinks of Russia! Our women won't be safe on the streets. We never wanted this camp in here. White men are no good in our business. We like our Mexicans. They don't complain; they live where we put them, and they aren't forever organizing. As for those bulletins which they say we sent out to get those migrants here, they were the work of the Communist Party. We've spent four hundred dollars to check on it. The Reds are burrowing from within . . . you know how they work!"

Meanwhile, however, the Associated Farmers, harassed by the La Follette Senate Investigating Committee, have issued a "Declaration of Law and Order" to be posted in "conspicuous places" throughout Imperial Valley. The declaration reads in part:

> This organization will use all its power and influence for the protection:

> *First*, of the lawful rights of every man to join and be active in any labor organization he chooses.

> *Second*, the right of every man to choose his own representatives for collective bargaining.

Of course, the declaration also emphasizes the "right of every man to refuse to join a union," and there are other loopholes for reaction. But the Declaration concludes: "Lawlessness and Mob Violence are things of the Past!" This means, among other things, that the days of the Vigilantes are over. They may still call the migrants Communists, but they are, none of them, anxious to make an issue of it. Occasionally, an Associated Farmer refuses to employ residents of a government camp in his fields, but most of them have learned that healthy men and children pick faster than the half-dead kind do. Finally, with the example set by the government camps continually before them, none but the most vicious and insensitive growers have failed to clean up those privately maintained "Hoovervilles" which threatened to become the scourge of the entire state. In short, grower opposition is on the wane. Recently, however, the Associated Farmers threatened to boycott all out-state pickers.

Another factor which has encouraged friendly relations between the Farm Security camps and surrounding communities is economic. Several months after the Brawley camp started, a delegation of merchants from nearby Calipatria asked the authorities for a similar camp. Figures show that Brawley merchants have benefited by approximately $16,000 a year through the presence of the Federal camp. Opposition was also quieted by a Government contribution of $13,000 for a share of Brawley's water supply.

Finally, the ordinary citizen has discovered that his town has been made a livelier place in which to live, with three or four hundred healthy mid-westerners within shouting distance. In Brawley, for instance, the camp puts on an old fashioned square dance every Saturday night. The camp orchestra from Indio took first prize at the Imperial County Fair. There are Friday night boxing matches in which the town boys often participate. The migrants' baseball teams are included in various sectional leagues. Famous people—movie actors and actresses—often visit the camp. As one Brawley lad put it: "Them Okies has sure pepped things up around here!"

All in all, the idea sponsored by Rexford Tugwell and Tom Collins, aided by Paul Taylor's tireless research has proved its mettle. The merchants, the police, and the health authorities aren't kicking. For many "Okies" this government camp is the first taste of real democracy. Theirs is a collective life, with plenty of outlets for individualism. The camp councils, two men and two women, are solving the little problems of every-day democracy without benefit of police or Vigilantes. Those men at the Arvia Camp to whom the Government has entrusted three-fifths of an acre apiece know the meaning and the necessity of production for use. In short, these lonely, drought-stricken migrants, under the guidance of humane and liberal men and women, are standing on the threshold of a new order, breaking ground for a civilization that nothing can stop. That's why the Associated Farmers still hate them. That's why bewildered men and women come from miles around to ask questions of people who have their fingers crossed, who aren't talking.

# CHAPTER TWO

# POWER, AUTHORITY, AND GOVERNANCE: FDR AND THE NEW DEAL

**From "Outlining the New Deal Program"**
*A fireside chat by Franklin D. Roosevelt,*
*broadcast by radio to the American public*
*May 7, 1933*

*Franklin Delano Roosevelt was born into a wealthy family in 1882, a distant cousin of the twenty-sixth president, Theodore Roosevelt. FDR practiced law, was elected to the New York State Senate, and served as assistant secretary of the U.S. Navy in the administration of President Woodrow Wilson (1912–1920). He went on to become the Democratic Party's vice presidential nominee in 1920 and later served as the two-term Progressive governor of New York (1928–1932). His crowning achievement was being elected four times to the presidency of the United States (1932–1945), leading America through the dark years of both the Great Depression and World War II (1939–1945).*

*An astute politician and a remarkable man, FDR seemed to be the kind of leader his country needed most in such perilous times. The Hoover administration had felt it prudent to move slowly in fixing the shattered U.S. economy, but FDR was a man of action who had promised Americans a*

*"New Deal" upon his election. That was a promise he was*
*determined to keep, no matter what the financial or political*
*cost would be. FDR kept the public informed of his ongoing*
*actions through a series of radio addresses that came to be*
*known as "fireside chats." The following fireside chat intro-*
*duced Americans to FDR's New Deal.*

———□———

On a Sunday night a week after my Inauguration I used the
radio to tell you about the banking crisis and the measures we
were taking to meet it. I think that in that way I made clear to
the country various facts that might otherwise have been misun-
derstood and in general provided a means of understanding
which did much to restore confidence.

Tonight, eight weeks later, I come for the second time to
give you my report—in the same spirit and by the same
means to tell you about what we have been doing and what
we are planning to do.

Two months ago we were facing serious problems. The
country was dying by inches. It was dying because trade and
commerce had declined to dangerously low levels; prices for
basic commodities were such as to destroy the value of the
assets of national institutions such as banks, savings banks,
insurance companies, and others. These institutions, because
of their great needs, were foreclosing mortgages, calling
loans, refusing credit. Thus there was actually in process of
destruction the property of millions of people who had borrowed money on that property in terms of dollars which had
had an entirely different value from the level of March, 1933.
That situation in that crisis did not call for any complicated

consideration of economic panaceas or fancy plans. We were faced by a condition and not a theory.

There were just two alternatives: The first was to allow the foreclosures to continue, credit to be withheld and money to go into hiding, and thus forcing liquidation and bankruptcy of banks, railroads and insurance companies and a re-capitalizing of all business and all property on a lower level. This alternative meant a continuation of what is loosely called "deflation," the net result of which would have been extraordinary hardship on all property owners and, incidentally, extraordinary hardships on all persons working for wages through an increase in unemployment and a further reduction of the wage scale.

It is easy to see that the result of this course would have not only economic effects of a very serious nature but social results that might bring incalculable harm. Even before I was inaugurated I came to the conclusion that such a policy was too much to ask the American people to bear. It involved not only a further loss of homes, farms, savings and wages but also a loss of spiritual values—the loss of that sense of security for the present and the future so necessary to the peace and contentment of the individual and of his family. When you destroy these things you will find it difficult to establish confidence of any sort in the future. It was clear that mere appeals from Washington for confidence and the mere lending of more money to shaky institutions could not stop this downward course. A prompt program applied as quickly as possible seemed to me not only justified but imperative to our national security. The Congress, and when I say Congress I mean the members of both political parties, fully understood this and gave me generous and intelligent support. The members of Congress realized that the methods of normal times had to be replaced in the emergency by measures which were suited to the serious and pressing requirements of the moment. There was no actual surrender of power, Congress still retained its constitutional authority and no one has the slightest desire to change the balance of these powers. The function of Congress is to decide what has to be done and to select the appropriate agency to carry out its will. This policy it has strictly adhered to. The only thing that has been happening has been to designate the President as the agency to carry out certain of the purposes of the Congress. This was constitutional and in keeping with the past American tradition.

The legislation which has been passed or in the process of enactment can properly be considered as part of a well-grounded plan.

First, we are giving opportunity of employment to one-quarter of a million of the unemployed, especially the young men who have dependents, to go into the forestry and flood prevention work. This is a big task because it means feeding, clothing and caring for nearly twice as many men as we have in the regular army itself. In creating this civilian conservation corps we are killing two birds with one stone. We are clearly enhancing the value of our natural resources and second, we are relieving an appreciable amount of actual distress. This great group of men have entered upon their work on a purely voluntary basis, no military training is involved and we are conserving not only our natural resources but our human resources. One of the great values to this work is the fact that it is direct and requires the intervention of very little machinery.

Second, I have requested the Congress and have secured action upon a proposal to put the great properties owned by our Government at Muscle Shoals [Alabama] to work after long years of wasteful inaction, and with this a broad plan for the improvement of a vast area in the Tennessee Valley. It will add to the comfort and happiness of hundreds of thousands of people and the incident benefits will reach the entire nation.

Next, the Congress is about to pass legislation that will greatly ease the mortgage distress among the farmers and the home owners of the nation, by providing for the easing of the burden of debt now bearing so heavily upon millions of our people.

Our next step in seeking immediate relief is a grant of half a billion dollars to help the states, counties and municipalities in their duty to care for those who need direct and immediate relief.

In addition to all this, the Congress also passed legislation authorizing the sale of beer in such states as desired. This has already resulted in considerable reemployment and, incidentally, has provided much needed tax revenue.

Now as to the future:

We are planning to ask the Congress for legislation to enable the Government to undertake public works, thus stimulating directly and indirectly the employment of many others in well-considered projects.

Further legislation has been taken up which goes much more fundamentally into our economic problems. The Farm

Relief Bill seeks by the use of several methods, alone or together, to bring about an increased return to farmers for their major farm products, seeking at the same time to prevent in the days to come disastrous over-production which so often in the past has kept farm commodity prices far below a reasonable return. This measure provides wide powers for emergencies. The extent of its use will depend entirely upon what the future has in store.

Well-considered and conservative measures will likewise be proposed which will attempt to give to the industrial workers of the country a more fair wage return, prevent cut-throat competition and unduly long hours for labor, and at the same time to encourage each industry to prevent over-production.

One of our bills falls into the same class, the Railroad Bill. It seeks to provide and make certain definite planning by the railroads themselves, with the assistance of the Government, to eliminate the duplication and waste that is now resulting in railroad receiverships and in continuing operating deficits.

I feel very certain that the people of this country understand and approve the broad purposes behind these new governmental policies relating to agriculture and industry and transportation. We found ourselves faced with more agricultural products than we could possibly consume ourselves and surpluses which other nations did not have the cash to buy from us except at prices ruinously low. We found our factories able to turn out more goods than we could possibly consume, and at the same time we have been faced with a falling export demand. We have found ourselves with more facilities to transport goods and crops than there were goods and crops to be transported. All of this has been caused in large part by a complete failure to understand the danger signals that have been flying ever since the close of the World War. The people of this country have been erroneously encouraged to believe that they could keep on increasing the output of farm and factory indefinitely and that some magician would find ways and means for that increased output to be consumed with reasonable profit to the producer.

But today we have reason to believe that things are a little better than they were two months ago. Industry has picked up, railroads are carrying more freight, farm prices are better, but I am not going to indulge in issuing proclamations of over-enthusiastic assurance. We cannot ballyhoo ourselves back to prosperity. I am going to be honest at all times with the people of the country. I do not want the people of this country to take the foolish course of letting this improvement come back on another speculative wave. I do not want the people to believe that because of unjustified optimism we can resume the ruinous practice of increasing our crop output and our factory output in the hope that a kind providence will find buyers at high prices. Such a course may bring us immediate and false prosperity but it will be the kind of prosperity that will lead us into another tailspin.

It is wholly wrong to call the measure that we have taken Government control of farming, control of industry, and control of transportation. It is rather a partnership between Government and farming and industry and transportation, not partnership in profits, for the profits would still go to the citizens, but rather a partnership in planning and partnership to see that the plans are carried out . . .

We are working toward a definite goal, which is to prevent the return of conditions which came very close to destroying what we call modern civilization. The actual accomplishment of our purpose cannot be attained in a day. Our policies are wholly within purposes for which our American Constitutional Government was established one hundred and fifty years ago.

I know that the people of this country will understand this and will also understand the spirit in which we are undertaking this policy. I do not deny that we may make mistakes of procedure as we carry out the policy. I have no expectation of making a hit every time I come to bat. What I seek is the highest possible batting average, not only for myself but for the team. Theodore Roosevelt once said to me: "If I can be right seventy-five per cent of the time I shall come up to the fullest measure of my hopes." . . .

Hand in hand with the domestic situation which, of course, is our first concern, is the world situation, and I want to emphasize to you that the domestic situation is inevitably and deeply tied in with the conditions in all of the other nations of the world. In other words, we can get, in all probability, a fair measure of prosperity return in the United States, but it will not be permanent unless we get a return to prosperity all over the world.

In the conferences which we have held and are holding with the leaders of other nations, we are seeking four great objectives. First, a general reduction of armaments and through this the removal of the fear of invasion and armed attack, and, at the same time, a reduction in armament costs, in order to help in the balancing of government budgets and the reduction of taxation. Secondly, a cutting down of the trade barriers, in order to re-start the flow of exchange of crops and goods between nations. Third, the setting up of a stabilization of currencies, in order that trade can make contracts ahead. Fourth, the reestablishment of friendly relations and greater confidence between all nations.

Our foreign visitors these past three weeks have responded to these purposes in a very helpful way. All of the nations have suffered alike in this great depression. They have all reached the conclusion that each can best be helped by the common action of all. It is in this spirit that our visitors have met with us and discussed our common problems. The international conference that lies before us must succeed. The future of the world demands it and we have each of us pledged ourselves to the best joint efforts to that end.

To you, the people of this country, all of us, the members of the Congress and the members of this Administration owe a profound debt of gratitude. Throughout the depression you have been patient. You have granted us wide powers, you have encouraged us with a wide-spread approval of our purposes. Every ounce of strength and every resource at our command we have devoted to the end of justifying your confidence. We are encouraged to believe that a wise and sensible beginning has been made. In the present spirit of mutual confidence and mutual encouragement we go forward.

And in conclusion, my friends, may I express to the National Broadcasting Company and to the Columbia Broadcasting System my thanks for the facilities which they have made available to me tonight.

## Clergy Letter from Walter G. Procter to President Franklin D. Roosevelt
### October 10, 1935

I shall deem it a favor if you will write to me about conditions in your community. Tell me where you feel our government can better serve our people.

*—Letter from President Roosevelt to members of the clergy in America, September 24, 1935*

*It is often difficult for the president of the United States, sequestered in the White House and surrounded by supportive advisers, to directly observe the effects of his or her policies on average Americans. In order to gain a better understanding of how well his New Deal policies were working, President Franklin D. Roosevelt wrote to numerous clergy members across the country and asked them to report back to him on the state of their parishioners.*

*From New York to San Francisco and many towns and cities in between, the clergy complied with the president's request. The reply of one clergyman—Walter G. Procter, a Presbyterian pastor at the Mayer Chapel and Neighborhood House in Indianapolis, Indiana—appears in the following selection.*

———□———

October 10, 1935
Dear Mr. President:
Received your communication of September 23 requesting my views of conditions in my community.

Permit me at the outset to say that I am complying with your request for information and our reaction to the "new Social Legislation just enacted" with the same honesty and good faith as I feel sure your letter was sent to me and other ministers. The following expressions of my views are based not only on my own observation and conclusions, but on conversations with representative people of my Church and neighborhood.

In my capacity as pastor and superintendent of Mayer Chapel and Neighborhood House (Presbyterian) I come in daily contact with the under-privileged victims of this depression, administering relief and endeavoring in many ways to ameliorate their condition and to keep up their morale.

Miss Hannah Noone, the Trustee of Center Township, which embraces most of Indianapolis, informs me that she is caring for 11,000 families. Three thousand men are, or will be soon, working on public projects. The housing problem is serious, as very few owners are willing to accept the trustee's terms.

A number of the manufacturing plants around here have increased their forces, but no increase of pay. On the other hand I learn of a common practice of other concerns, who, when an employee is discharged or quits for any reason, divide[s] his or her work among the remaining employees with no increase of pay. Many of these men and girls are really overworked, but dare not protest. Jobs are too scarce.

Employers are demanding more and more the choice cuts of labor-men between twenty-one and forty, in some instances not over thirty-five. Those younger or older are refused work regardless of their needs or fitness.

We are noting more pronounced effects of malnutrition among our clinic babies as a result of the mothers' pre-natal insufficiency of nourishment, as well as the unpalatable monotony and inadaptability of the food during this period.

Now that Federal Aid has been withdrawn from the township we are bracing ourselves, as a privately supported institution, to meet the increasing needs of the distressed. We are apprehensive of adequate funds for this purpose. An increase of gifts look doubtful at this time.

The average individual desires to adequately provide for himself and family and to build up a reserve for emergencies—sickness, misfortune, unemployment, and for old age and death. But under the present economic and industrial set-up he is the victim of formidable and overwhelming forces and conditions over far-seeing plans, and against which he, as an individual, striving to accomplish as an individual, the above desirable purposes, finds himself pitifully helpless.

Things have reached a stage in our economic and social structure where society in its governmental capacity should exercise unprecedented functions and assure the security of the individual; to ally itself with the individual workers as against the greed and unscrupulousness, the ruthless competition, the brutal exercise of power and privilege of "rugged individualism" to which the battle is to the strong and the devil take the weak.

Society in its governmental capacity must, as things are, step in and rescue children, women and helpless men from exploitation, provide facilities for unemployment reserves in the form of insurance, and provision for old age.

In this connection I wrote to express my hearty approval of forcing individuals and corporations with super incomes to bear a larger share of the cost of relief and recovery. Society, including labor, has enriched them. They have received more than a fair share of the rewards of industry (others' industry). It is only just that they should be made to disgorge.

Things cannot go on indefinitely as they have been. They are bound to reach a breaking point. Human nature can endure much, but it ultimately reaches its limits, and that means revolution. Free men will finally revolt. The American worker—manual or brain—is not a dumb, brutalized serf. He is a man. He is emerging from the stage of dumb acquiescence in things as they have been. He is asking why should they continue? How come these conditions? Why should "opportunity" mean only opportunity for the privileged few to exploit the helpless many? What is the way out?

The recent "Social Security Legislation" is an attempt to partly meet the situation. A small step, but nevertheless a step in the right direction—the faint streaks of the dawn of the better day.

In my judgement we are inevitably working toward a socialistic State. Bound to, if we are to escape Fascism or Communism and retain our democratic form of Government.

I fully appreciate the unprecedented difficulties of your high office at this time of economic stress, and the splendid efforts you have put forth to ameliorate it, though I, with millions of others, cannot approve of the destruction and limitation of foodstuffs.

Please accept my highest regard.

Yours Most sincerely,
Walter G. Procter
Mayer Chapel
448 W. Norwood Street
Indianapolis, IN
October 10, 1935

## Letter from Lorena Hickok to Harry Hopkins Regarding the Tennessee Valley Authority (TVA) June 6, 1934

*On May 18, 1933, President Franklin D. Roosevelt signed into law the Tennessee Valley Authority Act, which created the Tennessee Valley Authority (TVA). The TVA was designed to improve the navigability of the Tennessee River, provide for flood control, plan reforestation and the improvement of marginal farm lands, and assist in the region's industrial and agricultural development. Running through seven states (Tennessee, Kentucky, Virginia, North Carolina, Georgia, Alabama, and Mississippi), the Tennessee River flowed through some of the poorest areas of the South, so the act gave the TVA a mandate to improve the economic and social well-being of the people along the river.*

*In 1933, presidential advisor Harry Hopkins asked former Associated Press journalist Lorena Hickok to report to*

*him on the state of the nation. Hickok, a close friend of*
*Eleanor Roosevelt, was in the Tennessee Valley during June*
*1934, and sent two reports to Hopkins recording her impres-*
*sion of the region's progress and the local reaction to the*
*TVA. The following is from the first of these reports.*

———□———

From Lorena Hickok
To Harry L. Hopkins
Florence, Alabama June 6, 1934

Dear Mr. Hopkins:

A Promised Land, bathed in golden sunlight, is rising out
of the grey shadows of want and squalor and wretchedness
down here in the Tennessee Valley these days.

Ten thousand men are at work, building with timber and
steel and concrete the New Deal's most magnificent project,
creating an empire with potentialities so tremendous and so
dazzling that they make one gasp. I knew very little about
the Tennessee Valley Authority when I came down here last
week. I spent part of my first day, in Knoxville, reading up on
it. I was almost as excited as I used to get over adventure
stories when I was a child. This IS an adventure!

Since then I have been traveling through the Valley and
the state—a couple of days in Knoxville, a trip to the Norris
dam and the town of Norris, a day's motoring across to
Nashville, stopping enroute to look over a subsistence homestead colony a few miles from the Valley, a day in Nashville, a
day's trip down here, visiting with farmers, relief workers,
county agents in little towns along the way.

Today I saw the Wilson dam and went down into the power house—which is the best way, I found, to get an idea of how big this thing really is—and drove 20 miles on up the river to watch workmen drilling in rock to lay the foundations of the Wheeler dam.

I've talked with people who are doing this job, with people who live in the towns and cities that are going to feel the effects of this program, with ordinary citizens, with citizens on relief—as many kinds of people as I could find.

They don't all get so excited about it as I do. They criticize some features of the program. I have an impression that thousands of people right here in the Valley don't really know what it is all about. But the people—the people as a whole—are beginning to "feel" already the presence of TVA, even though it hasn't made any dent on our relief rolls.

Nearly 10,000 men—about 9,500—are at work in the Valley now, at Norris and Wheeler dams, on various clearing and building projects all over the area.

Thousands of them are residents of the Valley, working five and a half hours a day, five days a week, for a really LIVING wage. Houses are going up for them to live in—better houses than they have ever had in their lives before. And in their leisure time they are studying—farming, trades, the art of living, preparing themselves for the fuller lives they are to lead in that Promised Land.

You are probably saying, "Oh, come down to earth!" But that's the way the Tennessee Valley affects one these days.

Ten thousand men at work may not seem like so many when Tennessee still has a relief case load of 68,000 and

Alabama around 80,000. But it's something. And there's no "white collar problem" in Knoxville these days. And people say to you, "Oh, we're lucky down here in Tennessee. TVA's a help!"

"Oh, I haven't heard anybody say anything about the Depression for three months," remarked a taxicab driver in Knoxville the other day. "Business is three times as good as it was a year ago. You ought to see the crowds at the ballgames."

Over in Nashville the attitude seems to be:

"Maybe we don't get so direct a benefit out of TVA as they get in Knoxville, but it will be coming eventually. And in the meantime, at least, Roosevelt is trying. He's doing something!"

Another way by which people hereabouts are being made aware of TVA is in the lowering of rates for electricity. They've been forced down already, even where the distribution is still in the hands of privately owned companies.

"I put in an electric hot water heater sometime ago," one man told me, "but I haven't been able to use it because it cost too much. But now, with this new rate, I can. I can run that, with all my other equipment—range, iron, mangle [a machine that presses and irons laundry], vacuum cleaner, lights, and radio—for the same cost as I went without it before."

Before I leave the Valley, I'm going down to Tupelo, Miss., the first town to start buying its electric power directly from TVA, and see how they get along. Up here, one hears enthusiastic reports.

Well . . . Tennessee has got a huge job of rehabilitation on her hands. And with TVA setting up standards in rehabilitation, the rest of the state has got a long, long way to go.

Out of nearly 70,000 families on relief in Tennessee, probably 30,000 or more live in small towns or in the country. Many of these are in abandoned lumber and mining camps. Most of them who are farmers apparently are living on submarginal or marginal land.

Fairly typical, for Western Tennessee, I gather, was a district I visited yesterday. Table land. Thin soil. Terrible housing. Illiteracy. Evidence of prolonged undernourishment. No knowledge of how to live decently or farm profitably if they had decent land.

"Five years is about as long as you can get any crop on this land," one farmer told me. "Then it's gone and you have to clear some more and start over again."

Crops grown on it are stunted. Corn, for instance, grows only about a third as tall there as it does in Iowa. They tell me it isn't even good timber land. Just a thin coating of soil over rock. A county agent said it might make good orchard land, but any farming operation there should be under skilled supervision with authority to make farmers do as they were told.

Eastern Tennessee is worse, of course. There you see constantly evidence of what happens when you cut timber off mountain sides and plant crops there. There are great "bald patches" of rock on those mountains!

What to do with these people makes a nice little problem. Whether to move them off—and, if so, where to put them—or, on table land, for instance, where with careful and authoritative supervision they might eke out a living, leave them there and take a chance on their being absorbed in the

industries that should be attracted down here by the cheap
power furnished by TVA.

There might be, I should think, the possibility of a sort of
temporary supervision. Rehabilitate the present adult generation where they are. Try out orchards instead of corn on the
table land, for instance. And have it understood that their children are not to inherit that land, but that it will be taken over
by the Government as they die, the Government to pay the heirs
for it, either with cash or land somewhere else. The idea was
advanced by Grace Falke, Secretary Tugwell's assistant
[Rexford Tugwell, assistant secretary in the Agriculture
Department under FDR], who has joined me on this trip. Help
the parents to get at least a fairly decent living now and do a
bang-up job of public health and education on the children.

This may sound wild, but I doubt if in Tennessee there is
enough good land available for all of them.

Near Crossville, for instance, a subsistence homestead
unit, with some of the loveliest little houses you ever saw, is
being set up on about 12,000 acres of new land. They are starting out to raise mostly vegetables on it. The farm expert in
charge [says that the soil] won't stand up under anything heav-
ier, although it's good soil if handled expertly. They haven't been
able to dig cellars under those houses because, if you go down
20 inches below the surface, you hit rock! I wonder if any sort of
farming can ever be carried on permanently on soil that thin.

That homestead unit has the nicest houses I've seen any-
where. They are building them of a beautifully colored rock
found on the place. They are grand houses, really. But it's the
same old story. Each family moving in there will be somewhere

around $2,500 in debt, and any definite plans for enabling those people to pay off those debts aren't in evidence. They seem to be trusting to God—and the Government.

Well—so far, Tennessee hasn't got far with any rural rehabilitation program. As you know, they've had a lot of administrative trouble.

They've at last got a rural rehabilitation man, out of the agricultural extension service. He's just finding himself. They're not thinking of rural rehabilitation in Tennessee for this year, but next year.

And all over the state, in the rural areas, the story is the same—an illiterate, wretched people, undernourished, with standards of living so low that, once on relief, they are quite willing to stay there the rest of their lives. It's a mess.

But then—there's TVA. It's coming along. My guess is that, whatever they do or don't do about rural rehabilitation down in Tennessee, in another decade you wouldn't know this country. And the best part of it is that here the Government will have control. There's a chance to create a new kind of industrial life, with decent wages, decent housing. Gosh, what possibilities! You can't feel very sorry for Tennessee when you see that in the offing.

## "'Social Security' Under the New Deal"
### By Abraham Epstein
### From The Nation
### September 15, 1935

*Prior to the passage of the Social Security Act in 1935, the handicapped and the retired in America had no federal agency to which they could turn for assistance. Literally millions of dependent individuals were left to fend for themselves or rely on private charities.*

*The immediate effect of Social Security was startling: some 1.5 million elderly, handicapped, and dependent children began receiving cash allowances, while public health programs were expanded and strengthened in all forty-eight states. But those who benefited most from Social Security were retired American. Beginning on January 1, 1936, 26 million workers became eligible for retirement benefits, providing them with a more secure life in their golden years. Despite these tangible benefits, however, Social Security was born in chaos and riddled by controversy from the outset. Abraham Epstein, a leading advocate for old-age security, describes the difficult and troubled birth of Social Security in this 1935 article from* The Nation.

——□——

The social-security bill was signed by the President on August 14 with a succession of pens and under flood lights—as if to make up for the previous lack of publicity accorded it. Never before in the history of this or any other country has a bill of such great scope and import been passed with public opinion in such a daze about the issues. Unfortunately the present law seems doomed from the start by its complex, slovenly, and mangled character. The subject of social insurance, in which economics, politics, statistics, social policy, trade unionism, wages, and industrial production are intertwined, was barely discussed in the United States prior to the President's message to Congress in June, 1934, when he promised to undertake "the great task of furthering the security of the citizen and his family through social insurance." For more than half a century social-insurance programs have been keen political issues throughout Europe, but here there has not been even academic interest; our newspapers gave the subject no notice until a year ago and have given it very little since. Everywhere abroad social-insurance measures have been championed chiefly by organized labor. Our labor movement has either opposed them or given half-hearted and uninformed support.

No wonder, therefore, that the President's speech of June 8, 1934, fell like a bombshell on the country. The most ardent advocates of social insurance in America were bewildered by its boldness and political audacity. Even more deluding was the almost universal approval which greeted the speech. Everybody jumped on the social-security bandwagon. Governors made it their campaign issues. Congressmen spoke for it. Candidates for state legislatures made it a plank in their platforms. Even candidates for city councils and sheriff's offices felt compelled to declare themselves in favor of social security. And when, on November 6, 1934, the American electorate gave the President the most Democratic Congress in two generations, hopes were raised sky-high.

Like all nine days' wonders, it was too good to be true. The President spoke of "social security," and who could be against that? True, he did mention "social insurance," but why bother to discover the meaning of so strange a term? Of several hundred articles and newspaper stories on social security appearing during the past year, less than a score attempted an analysis of social insurance. Social security was identified with old-age pensions, for an ardent twenty-year campaign for old-age security had brought about a tremendous popular demand for old-age protection. More than half the states had actually adopted pension laws. This movement had gained such popularity that it attracted a galaxy of nondescript promoters ranging from the Fraternal Order of Eagles to the messianic Dr. Townsend [Dr. Francis E. Townsend, an early supporter of social security]. The country was thus clamoring for old-age pensions. But the Administration, symbolized by Madame Secretary [of Labor Frances] Perkins, seemed for a while almost totally unaware of this uproar. Miss Perkins had been principally concerned with the problem of unemployment insurance. As late as November 14, 1934, there was an attempt to confine the federal program to unemployment insurance. At that time the President, in a speech admittedly prepared under Miss Perkins's supervision, said, "I do not know whether this is the time for any federal legislation on old-age security."

This conflict in basic objectives marked only the beginning of the confusion. Difficulties were inherent in the very make-up of the President's Committee on Economic Security. For in creating a committee to study this subject and prepare legislation, the President, instead of setting up an expert commission, entrusted the subject to five of his busiest Cabinet members, already driven to distraction by the many tasks of the New Deal program. The responsibility for formulating the concise and comprehensive legislation fell naturally upon the chairman of the committee, Miss Perkins. For one reason or another Miss Perkins ignored the recognized American students of the problem. A one-day circus was staged in Washington on November 14 with over 300 "experts" in attendance and with the formal speeches so arranged as to frustrate one another. A staff composed largely of complete novices in social insurance or of persons connected with some fringes of the problem was recruited to advise the Cabinet committee. There were also a Technical Advisory Committee of office-holders, government office-holders, some fourteen other committees, and an Advisory Council of prominent representatives of the public, employers, and workers.

The direction of the committee's staff came exclusively from the chairman of the Cabinet committee. Since Miss Perkins had no particular panacea for old-age dependency, the staff was comparatively free to work out this phase of the program. Had their recommendations been followed, we might have had a constructive method of meeting the problem of old-age dependency. But Miss Perkins had a palliative for unemployment. Early in 1934 she sponsored the Wagner-Lewis bill providing for the encouragement of unemployment insurance through the tax-offset method. This involved a federal tax on employers' payrolls throughout the nation, to be remitted to employers who paid a duplicating tax under state unemployment-insurance systems.

When, after the nation's reaction to the President's speech of November 14, it became clear that action on old-age security could not be postponed, old-age pensions were added to the security program. Since the old opponents of labor legislation were busy fighting the NRA and other New Deal activities, their opposition to the measure was palsied. They were also convinced that it was useless to fight the swelling tide of enthusiasm for old-age pensions, and they were not much worried about the cumbersome tax-offset method proposed, since they felt this would either be held unconstitutional or prove so complicated and irksome as to nullify itself. There remained only the question of health insurance. Here the reactionary American Medical Association got busy at once and succeeded in suppressing any suggestion for health insurance made by the Cabinet committee, as well as the committee's staff report on health insurance, promised for March 15, 1935.

The Administration had probably never dreamed that it would have to do more for old-age security than establish a system of federal subsidies to states enacting standardized pension laws. Such bills had been before Congress for many years, and committees in two successive Congresses had reported them favorably. This legislation would have passed the Seventy-third Congress had not the President promised a more comprehensive program for 1935. But when the Cabinet committee learned of the future expense involved—considerably exaggerated by the staff because of unfamiliarity with the problem—it endorsed the logical plan of instituting simultaneously a system of contributory compulsory old-age insurance. Although handicapped by a total lack of information on a subject requiring years of study, the staff did draft a reasonable plan, which was approved by the Cabinet committee and incorporated in the original bill.

This plan provided for payroll contributions from employers and employees to reach two and one-half percent each within the next twenty years. Pensions to all insured were to begin in 1942 out of money borrowed from the accumulated fund. After thirty or thirty-five years the federal government

was to reimburse the loan. But when the President learned
that the federal government would owe the fund more than a
billion dollars by 1970 he ordered his Secretary of the
Treasury—a member of the Cabinet committee, who apparently
had approved this scheme before it was introduced—to insist
that under no circumstances would the federal government
assume any financial responsibility. The plan must be made
self-sustaining.

Under White House pressure the House committee
stepped up the contributions to a total of 6 percent within
twelve years. This transfers the entire burden of old-age
dependency after 1942 to the backs of the young workers and
their employers, to the exclusion of the well-to-do, who have
shared in the maintenance of the aged poor since the establishment of the Elizabethan poor-law system three centuries
ago. Since industry will make every effort to pass on its
levy to the consumers, it means that the young employees—
in their dual role of workers and consumers—will bear the
major cost of the accumulated problem of old-age dependency.
No other nation has ever put into operation a plan of this
nature without government contributions derived from the
higher-income groups.

The old-age contributory insurance plan is fraught
with many other dangers. Enormous reserves, estimated at
more than $10,000,000,000 by 1948 and at more than
$40,000,000,000 in 1980, are contemplated. These will create
a stupendous problem of investment. Experience everywhere
indicates that politicians will hardly be able to keep their
hands off such easy money. The cold-storaging of so much

sorely needed purchasing power not only frustrates the expressed aims of the New Deal but may definitely hamper recovery. The constitutionality of the entire scheme is also extremely doubtful.

In the matter of unemployment insurance the staff's task was even more onerous. Despite violent criticism no other plan except the tax-offset method was countenanced. When the staff's expert on unemployment insurance opposed this plan as ineffective, he was promptly dismissed. His report was never published. Every effort was artfully made to have the Advisory Council endorse the tax-offset method. This body also was ignored and dismissed as of no further use when, after careful deliberation, all the representatives of the employers and of organized labor and some of the outstanding members of the public decided by majority vote against this plan. Only the clumsy, duplicating tax-offset method permitting individual company reserves and making possible a miscellany of forty-eight contradictory state laws with grave constitutional difficulties was permitted to emerge.

The work of the Cabinet committee was shrouded in mystery until the day the bill was introduced. It was prepared in great haste by an inexperienced young Harvard graduate without consultation either with students of the problem or the experienced Congressional draftsmen. It is even doubtful whether all the members of the Cabinet committee examined it. So incompetently and loosely drawn was the bill that its introduction caused a sensation. Although it was completely unintelligible, Administration impatience rushed Congressional hearings at which official spokesmen attempted to explain away the meaninglessness of the drafted bill. Administration spokesmen consumed more than 1,000 of the nearly 2,500 pages of testimony in both houses. Only after these spokesmen were through were others who persisted in their attempts allowed to speak. The House Ways and Means Committee attempted to limit all outside witnesses to five minutes and on one occasion forcibly ejected a Communist spokesman when he overstepped the time limit—a procedure unknown in Congress in many years.

The House committee could not proceed with the bill as presented and ordered its draftsmen to make it intelligible. The latter, unable properly and constitutionally to retain the unemployment-insurance provisions permitting all kinds of individual schemes, limited all state plans to the pooled fund. Angered by the slipshod job presented to it, the committee took the Social Security Administration Board out of the Department of Labor and made it independent. Outside of the contributory old-age insurance plan insisted upon by the White House and the questionable tax-offset scheme the House bill was sound in its federal grants to states for the aged, dependent mothers, and child welfare.

The proponents of social insurance were encouraged by the improvements made in the House. They looked forward to the removal of other faulty features in the Senate. But this was not to be. The Administration was insistent, and few members in either house had time to master the lengthy and complicated bill covering ten different subjects. Convinced that the Administration's choice was "all or nothing," they made up their mind to vote for all. Thus during five full days of Senate discussion not even half a column of the Congressional Record

was devoted to the prodigious and unprecedented scheme of
unemployment insurance, outside of explanatory remarks by
the committee chairman and Senator [Robert] Wagner
[Democratic senator from New York], the sponsor of the bill.
The economically unwise and socially menacing contributory
old-age insurance plan was given less than a column in the
hundreds of pages of Congressional debate, and that only
toward the very end. Only its constitutionality was thoroughly
discussed. Senator after Senator declared that this part of the
bill is unconstitutional but no one made an effort to amend it
to avoid nullification. During the debate on the Clark amendment to exempt private pension schemes from contributory
insurance a number of Senators pointed out that this would
further complicate the constitutional difficulties. To this
Senator [Joel Bennett "Champ"] Clark [Democrat from
Missouri] replied in typical vein: "The constitutionality of the
proposed act is already so doubtful that it would seem to me to
be a work of supererogation to bring up the question of constitutionality in regard to the pending amendment."

The Senate bill not only differed much from the original
proposal but destroyed every improvement made in the House.
The Clark amendment further ruined the old-age contributory
plan. The House improvements on unemployment insurance
were wiped out by restoring most of the original questionable
provisions. Even the simple subsidy plans were undermined by
the Russell amendment granting federal pensions in states
which have no pensions as yet, thereby pitching the entire
subject into the political arena and halting state action for old-
age security. At the insistence of the House conferees the

Clark amendment was eliminated and the Social Security Board, which the Senate had reinstated in the Department of Labor, was again made independent.

The United States thus possesses a new Social Security Act, just as a short while ago it also possessed a National Industrial Recovery Act and a Railroad Retirement Act. Its fate now lies with the courts. The federal grants for pensions in old age, to dependent mothers, to the blind, and to varied child-welfare and public-health activities are sound and constitutional. They mark truly advanced steps and genuine progress. The unemployment-insurance and old age contributory insurance plans, however, are administratively and socially unwise.

The effect this bill may have on the American social-insurance movement is of vital importance. Social insurance is recognized today as offering the only practicable instrument for meeting the problem of insecurity arising from modern industrial development. It is used in communist as well as capitalist and fascist countries. Its chief asset lies in its power to distribute the cost over all groups in society—the rich as well as the poor. But in placing the entire burden of insecurity upon the workers and industry, to the exclusion of the well-to-do in the nation, the present social-security bill violates the most essential modern principles of social insurance. There is also grave danger that the administrative perplexities inherent in the bill, to say nothing of possible court nullification, may deal a death blow to the entire movement in the United States.

# CHAPTER THREE

# INDIVIDUALS, GROUPS, AND INSTITUTIONS: THE PERILS AND PROMISE OF THE NEW DEAL

**"Caught in the Trough"**
**By Anonymous**
**From the Atlantic Monthly**
**June 1932**

Not everyone living during the Great Depression became so desperately poor that they faced hunger and homelessness. Members of the middle class were not so well off, however, that they did not feel the economic pinch. Indeed, many urban and suburban Americans of the late 1920s were living relatively comfortable, though far from extravagant, middle-class existences. But the Depression took its toll on them, as well, turning once secure lifestyles into a daily struggle against poverty and for continued membership in the middle class.

The government did what it could for these citizens by instituting low-interest home loans, banking regulations to protect what small personal savings might remain, and such programs as Social Security. But for all the efforts of the Roosevelt administration, the Depression remained a period of intense hardship for all but the richest Americans,

*as attested to by this anonymous first-person account of a*
*middle-class family teetering on the brink of poverty.*

———□———

# I

For the first time in my life I am facing financial insecurity of
the sort that I had always supposed people of the middle
classes must escape by virtue of good blood, gentle breeding,
and adequate education. My father is a college professor in
comfortable circumstances. My maternal grandfather was a
lawyer who enjoyed more than a degree of antebellum pres-
tige, my paternal grandfather a physician and gentleman
planter of the Old South. My mother and father were both left
patrimonies sufficient to provide their children with luxuries
and educational opportunities in excess of those a professor's
salary would warrant. I was graduated from one of the large
Eastern colleges, received my Master's degree from the
University of Chicago, traveled abroad for the finishing touch
my parents prescribed, taught in the history department of a
woman's college for three years, and in 1920 married a man
whose future seemed secured by connection with a legal firm
of good standing.

For nine years our income rose steadily—from $3000 in
1920 to about $7000 in 1929. Even with this salary, saving
was not easy. At first there were the expenses incident to the
birth of two babies. Then there were the clubs my husband
joined because he was urged to do so by his employers, who
looked to the widened contacts a young associate might bring
to the firm. It seemed important that we should live in a good
part of the city. Because my training had not been of a domestic

sort, I felt that I could not do without a maid in the children's infancy. Still, during the first years we kept up a $20,000 life-insurance policy and by the beginning of 1929 had about $2000 in 6 per cent bonds.

It was then that we bought a house in the suburbs. The two older lawyers had made my husband a junior partner with a 20 per cent interest in the earnings, which, according to the net income of the year before, promised to be about $8000. It did not seem extravagant, therefore, to buy a house that cost $15,000. Our savings made the first payment. The house was financed by a $9000 first mortgage and a second mortgage of $4000, payable in installments of fifty dollars a month. The ninety-five dollars we were assuming in interest and curtail-ments was only twenty dollars in excess of the rent we had been paying, and a large part of it could be interpreted in terms of savings.

But there were expenses which had not entered into our reckonings. The car that had been serving us for some time had to be replaced. In the suburbs one must have shrubs and a garden; and, when a house is built on a hillside, there must be grading and retaining walls. Outdoor expenses that seemed to us necessary came to $1000. The sum of $750 went at once for new furniture, curtains, and draperies. To cap it all, that year the earnings of the firm fell off sharply. Instead of the $8000 my husband had expected, his income was but $7000. It was a close squeeze for us, but we man-aged to finish the year 1929 without going into debt. We had a house and garden that represented the expenditure of $16,000, in which we figured our equity at $3600; our car and furniture had no liens against them; but there was no money in the savings bank.

## II

Almost at once the depression gathered momentum. Several mergers and failures took from my husband's firm clients whose retaining fees had been valuable considerations. Our income for 1930 decreased to $5000. With our living scaled to the larger amount, it was by dint of what we thought the strictest economy that we reached the end of the year without plunging into debt. We were not alarmed, however. Though there was much talk of hard times when our friends gathered in the evenings, there was little real pessimism. The country had passed through many such storms. Its seaworthiness was never questioned. On December 31 our neighbors gathered to bid farewell to one of the worst years America had ever seen and to welcome another that would surely bring a return of prosperity. No one mentioned the analogy between the depression and the days of stress that lasted from 1873 to 1878. That other post-war reaction was too far away to be remembered.

But prosperity did not come. Steadily the collections of my husband's firm decreased. Not only was 20 per cent of the profits inadequate to support our family, but business had fallen off to such an extent that the older members of the firm, who had built up its clientele, no longer needed an associate. During January and February of 1931 my husband drew $200 a month, and the first of March the partnership was dissolved by mutual consent. The first of April he secured a position in the legal department of a life-insurance company at a salary of

$200 a month, where the work was both uninteresting and without a future. At the end of each trying four weeks, however, we clutched our $200 with the grip of the drowning. My husband might have accepted the alternative of hanging out his shingle and starting afresh. The hazards seemed too great — what with the house on our hands and two children to feed and clothe and educate, and no liquid savings.

Our first thought, of course, was to sell the house and lower immediately the standard of living which had not seemed too high two years before. We hoped that we could salvage the $4350 that we had put into it and get the full $16,000 value. Gradually, however, we were forced to believe the real-estate agents, who told us that there was no purchaser at any price, and that houses were simply not being sold. Our offer to sell for $11,650, the sum covering the two liens, has brought no prospective customers. On the first of October a curtailment of $500 on the first mortgage was due. For a time there seemed no way to raise the necessary sum. Finally the holder of the second mortgage permitted us to increase our indebtedness to him by advancing the money for the curtailment.

The first of December my husband lost his position with the life-insurance company. The fault, admittedly, was not his. It merely became necessary to cut expenses and decrease the office force. At that moment the pittance which had been coming in with comforting regularity ceased abruptly and at the season when men were prating of peace on earth and good will toward men. For the sake of the children we maintained an outward semblance of Christmas merriment, while our hearts were filled with heavy forebodings.

Obviously there was nothing for my husband to do but open a law office of his own. First he did try to secure another position. He talked to his friends; he made inquiries of strangers. Had he been a day laborer, he could have applied to an agency. There seems to be no organization, however, that caters to the needs of professional men whose income has been $8000 a year and who are willing to do anything at any price. Besides, the professional man who has been trained to await the coming of business lacks the sort of initiative needed in such an emergency as that in which we found ourselves. Bankruptcy would be no solution of the problem, for our current bills are negligible, and nothing could lift from us the moral obligation to meet those second-mortgage notes, which are held by a man who has been gallant and understanding.

## III

We are now struggling along from day to day, in hand-to-mouth fashion, like Mr. Micawber. During the first three months of 1931, and particularly during the terrible month of March when nothing was coming in, we were forced to borrow upon our life-insurance policies to the full extent of their loan value, for we had not then adjusted ourselves to the economies that we later found possible. Although we are still living in an eight-room house, we have no domestic assistance except that furnished by a washerwoman who comes once a week.

If the salary in the legal department of the life-insurance company had continued, we might have managed to keep our heads above water, despite the loss of so large a part of our income. My husband cut the grass, worked the shrubs and flowers, and waxed the floors. I did the marketing at a cash-and-carry store, as well as the cooking and the cleaning. The ninety-five dollars that had to be found each month for interest and second-mortgage payments was an item as fixed as the orbit of the sun. We cut our other expenses to the bone. We spent thirty-five dollars a month for food, and miraculously stretched the remaining seventy dollars of my husband's salary to cover taxes, insurance premiums, and other household items such as telephone, electricity, gasoline, and fuel. I managed by means of part-time work and the twenty-five dollars a rented room brings in monthly to buy the essential clothes and incidentals and contribute to certain other unexpected expenses.

College teaching is the profession in which my training and experience lie. In my community there is no opening in a college. Even if our local school board were not prejudiced against employing married women in the high school, I could hardly undertake work so time-consuming when I am constantly needed by the children in the home. Consequently, I have found a modicum of tutoring, a bit of research work connected with a historical society, and have sold magazine articles based upon college theses. In all, I have averaged an income of about $100 a month—this since the beginning of last April.

In December 1931, my husband brought in nothing. In January, collections from a few small cases netted $116. We have no idea that February will yield anything like that much, and we do not know what we can depend on in the future. Since the children must be fed, payments on interest, insurance, and taxes have not been met. We have not been able to pay for the fuel oil bought in October. Yet in a few days we must ask for an extension of credit, for our supplies are practically exhausted. This situation would have seemed impossible a few years ago. Here we are, two people with college degrees, people of industry, training, and experiences about to qualify for the bread line! Whether I can continue to stand the strain of a sixteen-hour working day is problematic. Then, too, there is always the chance that, even if my health survives, the demand for my outside work may cease. Grueling labor performed without hope saps youth and energy and all the creative powers that come as the heritage of the normally endowed.

In the beginning we tried to continue the social activities in which we had always taken part, but the drain on time and resources proved too great. Now the extra expense of sandwiches and tea is prohibitive. To our mortification we have discovered how soon one can be forgotten when it is impossible to reciprocate social courtesies.

Yet we are too busy and too weary to miss our former pleasures a great deal. I love my home, with its shady side porch swept in summer by a gentle breeze; with its four airy bedrooms, chintz-hung and restful; with its spacious living room, where furniture is grouped pleasantly about a colonial mantel; with its sunny breakfast nook, its green and white kitchen, and its tiled baths. I love the log fire which is prolonging the life of that oil for which we have not paid.

On the other hand, I long to be freed of the burdens the house imposes. The expanse of floor space must be kept polished; little finger prints must constantly be wiped from white woodwork; nickel and brass and long mirrors must be bright and shiny. The old standard of living to which our lives have accustomed us is something of which we can never be rid. Even if there is no maid, meals must be conducted with a certain amount of decorum. Our morale requires that there be no letting down in those details that we hold as dear differentiations setting us apart from the great unwashed and unlettered multitudes.

So, abstractly and concretely, we are shackled to our traditions. Hours are consumed cleaning the ornate silver that came from a grandmother who used to consign its intricate pattern to the care of slaves, in dusting and polishing carved mahogany that is a beloved, though burdensome, heritage. Cumbered and fettered as we are, there is no chance for us to live easily on the day laborer's income. The ancestral furniture and silver now have small market value, even if we could bring ourselves to part with them. My diamond engagement ring would bring about twenty-five dollars from a pawnbroker, I am told. No antique dealer would offer a third of their value for my grandmother's highboy and love seats.

## IV

We have to fight on, sustained by the belief that our children may eventually reap the benefits of our endeavors. It is not only their material welfare that concerns us, no matter how driving are the tasks that each day presents. We must help them with their lessons in the evenings. We must guide their activities. We must direct their reading. Past generations are pressing upon us to equip generations yet to be. Our children must not be denied normal pleasures, must not be permitted to develop the sense of inferiority which small differentiations from their friends inevitably engender; they must live in a home open to their playmates, must not feel the strain that their parents cannot escape.

Besides, I am convinced that parsimony should not be instilled into them; they must be taught to assume their share of expenses without losing their self-respect. Though I was not reared in affluence, my childhood was free from financial worries. No one, so far as I know, in my husband's family or in mine ever set out deliberately to make money. Our progenitors belonged to the professional classes, who took more or less for granted enough wealth to provide the necessities and cultural advantages, enough to afford freedom from carking care. I do not remember in my youth ever hearing a discussion of ways and means. Consequently, one of the most unpleasant features of our present predicament is the dollar consciousness which has been forced upon us.

Perhaps the cultured middle group in America needed to be shaken out of its complacency. Yet, as complacency passes, something valuable is being lost along with it. This was the class that gave balance to the vulgar extremes of poverty and wealth, both of which exerted an enervating influence upon the social order. The results of this merging of the middle class with the lower must remain for time to show.

Within me an intermingling of Scotch and Irish blood is responsible for the feeling that, while big expenditures need not be made, it is degrading to indulge in penuriousness. My position may not be defensible, and I am not attempting to defend it. I am merely accepting and making the best of it.

My husband has passed the age when a new start in life is likely to meet with success. Younger men, if times ever get better, will no doubt have another chance. Older men, well established in their professions, may be able to hold fast till the country is on its feet again. My husband, caught in the trough at forty and looking ten years older than he did two years ago, will scarcely be able to pull himself out and start uphill again. His situation is like that of the college boys who enlisted during the World War and were never able to complete their education.

Looking back over the last decade, we have those regrets that are the product of hindsight. Buying the house in the suburbs was the cardinal mistake which we should like most to see undone. Yet, at the time, there were many to advise us to buy, and there was no Cassandra to warn of coming disasters. We believed that the purchase of the house would add to our financial stability, would prove an incentive to saving, and would provide a permanent home which would eventually be paid for. The little girl, who was pale and anemic, is now fat and rosy-cheeked. The boy is a finer, ruddier chap for the trees he has climbed. Though we may lose the savings that have gone into the house and carry for years the rest of those first-mortgage notes, nothing can take from us the good that has come to the children; whatever happens, they are starting life with splendid physiques.

While we have succeeded in keeping melancholy from touching these young lives, the children have not entirely escaped the new seriousness that has come upon us, and are satisfactorily assuming a share of responsibility. Certainly intensity of effort has drawn my husband and me closer together. Beneath the frank facing of facts and the ghastly undercurrent of fear which characterize our attitude toward the future, there is always the glimmer of hope. Perhaps, after all, there is some truth in the old stories of magic; perhaps there may be a fairy godmother who will some day wave her wand above us.

## From "Housing and Politics"
### By Charles Abrams
### From Survey Graphic
### February 1, 1940

*Depression-era families would sometimes be faced with a stark choice: buy food or pay their rent or mortgage. Often, there wasn't enough money for both. Affordable housing was scarce and often dangerous or unhealthy. The slum areas of cities, in which turn-of-the-century tenement buildings were equipped with antiquated sanitary systems and crowded with half a dozen or more people to a bedroom, expanded during the Depression. In the suburbs, middle-class Americans found themselves facing foreclosure of their homes (when banks take houses back after mortgage payments are not met). Rural America was suffering even worse. Farmers lost their farms and homes, while "hobos" (homeless wanderers) lived in shanties or slept in open fields as they roamed the countryside. Some of the first New Deal agencies created by Congress following President Franklin Roosevelt's legislative blitz in the earliest days of his presidency were designed to help find or create housing for America's*

*dispossessed. Charles Abrams, an author who would go on to
write* Forbidden Neighbors: A Study of Prejudice in Housing
*(1955), examines the threats posed by politics and an apathetic
and uninformed public to the New Deal's housing mission.*

————□————

The public and semi-public agencies responsible for housing,
soil conservation and rural resettlement are creatures of politics. Now, in 1940, a great program hangs in the balance as
political ears are close to the ground, trying to distinguish
between clamoring lobbies and the voice of the people. Voters,
take notice!

Throughout America's history the land question has
been a central problem, a burning issue. The acute forms in
which it confronts us now have been accumulating for a
century: land use, security of tenure, the plight of farmers,
sharecroppers, rural and urban slum dwellers, debt-burdened
home owners, the stability of the whole land economy itself.
In the last few years we have seen dramatic overtures in
these fields by the federal government which now owns two
fifths of all farm mortgage debt and one fifth of all urban
mortgage debt. AAA, FHA, USHA have all made tentative
stabs at the problems.

Today we have reached a crossroads where a choice
may have to be made. What have these experiments yielded?
What have these demonstrations demonstrated? Were the
housing projects designed only for the lucky few who got in
early, or is their construction to go on until every slum is
cleared? What of the labor camps, the communities for stranded
groups, the Greenbelt towns, the subsistence homesteads, the

farm-buying for migrant tenants and sharecroppers, the attempts at soil conservation and restoration—are these to continue until all are provided for, or are they, too, only demonstrations that have served their political purpose and are now to be abandoned?

The answers depend largely on the public attitude. But the public attitude will depend upon how much the public knows and how earnestly it makes itself felt as a result.

A well organized minority, not too strenuously opposed, can destroy even a deserving program where the public generally has evinced little concern over it. Not that public sympathy cannot be stirred. But it won't happen by itself. Public opinion must not only be roused to demand continuing action against the growing demand for "economy" in everything but war expenditures, but it must also be informed so that it does not mistake the shadow for the substance, does not accept a program of payments to absentee landlords in the guise of relief to farm tenants, does not accept tax exemption to private builders as a means of housing those of low income.

Low rent housing, resettlement, rural relief, soil conservation and reclamation, all these stand at the political crossroads today. The next few months may be decisive. What chance is there that public sentiment can lift these measures from their present position as experiments and stop-gaps into a realistic and adequate long range program?

There are a number of factors operating against such a development. For one thing, federal land policies are still linked in the public mind to the nightmare years that came after 1929.

The scales could be tipped and all the progress so far achieved wiped out by such developments as a major recovery or a high pressure economy drive.

Not even the persons for whom the benefits are intended give any large measure of concerted support. There is no such thing as a sharecroppers' movement, or a tenants' movement on an adequate scale. A few organizations do good work in canalizing public opinion on zoning and tenement reform, in resisting raids on housing authorities by established political groups, and in sponsoring legislation. But these are not "movements" in the same sense we might speak of the Labor movement or even of the "Ham-and-Eggs" or Townsend movements. It is one thing to organize veterans for a bonus drive or inspire our elders to seek a $50-a-week paradise. Regardless of the merits, victory would bring immediate and tangible benefit to the humblest follower. The inspiration and intensity of feeling of such drives are absent on the depressed plane of the sharecropper or the slum tenant. To them a housing project can only mean some slight increase in their infinitesimal chances of finally being picked as tenants.

## The Facts of Life

In seven cities referenda have been held during the past year to test the local attitude on public housing. In four the vote was favorable. In Flint, Michigan, in Portland, Oregon, and in Burlington, Vermont, it was unfavorable. In all cases the turnout for the vote was poor. In Flint, which needed workers' housing as much as any other city in the country, where the contrast between the modern General Motors factories and the archaic tumbledown human shelters furnish a sardonic commentary on modern life, less than twenty-five percent of the eligible voters participated. Opposition there, as in Portland and Burlington, was articulate and well organized. In New Britain, Connecticut, where housing just skimmed through, a combination of hardware manufacturers and mis-guided workers almost succeeded in depriving the city of housing. The workers who owned small houses had been told that they were sure to lose them if housing projects were built, while the manufacturers were afraid that the projects would become meeting places for CIO organizers. At some public meetings, supporters of housing were booed down, even by people in work shirts.

Yet, in spite of all these obstacles, the basis for a real housing movement exists. The newly completed projects have begun to attract a genuine sympathetic interest. The Los Angeles newspapers that recently boiled over when a federal official told them their slums were the worst in the country have now begun to look at their back streets. Opposition in Yonkers, N.Y., and Detroit, Michigan, is developing into keen curiosity as the actual construction proceeds. Two hundred local housing authorities have been formed in less than two years. The high courts of sixteen states have already upheld the purposes of housing authorities and the legality of tax exemp-tion on their projects. They have condemned slum conditions in opinions which, as human documents on the background and aims of public housing, can hardly be excelled.

It is clear that, in the face of intense opposition, there has got to be even more powerful support—support which can have an infinitely broader base provided the spearhead groups which always precede mass movements keep everlastingly at it. Every community has a potential nucleus for action— whether it is a housing council or a women's club or a church group. But it is not only emotional drive that is required. Housing is no longer an emotional issue alone. It has gone past that initial stage. Now, for its fullest measure of success, it requires public familiarity with techniques, procedures, alternatives, methods, norms and concepts. It requires a public able to distinguish substance from oratory, a public that must know not only why we need housing but what kind of housing, where, at what cost, for whom.

It must learn to recognize what are details, and what are fundamentals. When real estate organizations abandon their direct opposition to all housing, but insist that only slum clearance and re-housing on the same sites be allowed, then the social workers who have been insistent on the same thing must begin to realize the facts: that purchase by the government of certain high cost slum real estate bails out unlucky real estate investments and that it does little or nothing to combat the growing shortage of low rental houses of any kind. When, in 1938, a leading gubernatorial candidate in the East expressed great sympathy for the slum tenant but blasted the New Deal housing policy for invasion of states' rights, we must recognize that he meant an end to federal aid for housing, and that that in turn means the end of the whole housing program for the present. Only two or three states would make the large appropriations required, and our cities, their finances being what they are, certainly could not do it alone.

For the public must go even further than that. It must realize that adequate housing is possible only if the states and cities are ready to carry their end of the housing load. This means that Washington must not be expected to do everything and pay for everything. There must be enough non-federal projects, locally financed and state-aided, to supplement the necessarily inadequate federal program . . .

### *On All Fronts*

Action is required on two fronts now—local and federal. States should be made to follow. Locally there is the problem of freedom from favoritism and politics, for nothing will so soon discredit the movement as the impression that it furnishes an opportunity for favored contracts or for favored political henchmen either as officials or as tenants, the suspicion or prospect of "slum-mandering" by which a project is located in a hostile political district and then loaded with tenants who will vote "right." There is the need to see that the local council or selectmen or board of aldermen will grant the necessary funds for projects to proceed. Nationally, the problem is to make Congress see the fundamental importance of continuing the program it has begun, to make it really affect the pattern of our lives, so that we shall not be content merely with tantalizing experiments and models. Possibly we may even hope to succeed in making housing, land use control, soil reclamation an integral part of both party platforms as in England.

Difficult as the job is, a good many things have happened in the last few years to help make possible the creation of strong public backing. We have the challenging new communities themselves, incomparably better physically, socially, recreationally, than anything those of higher income have been able to achieve. We have the stirring and popular films such as *The City*, *The River*, *The Plough That Broke the Plains*. We have excellent traveling exhibits such as that of the Museum of Modern Art. John Steinbeck has written his heartrending best seller, *The Grapes of Wrath*.

In addition to an aroused and educated public opinion, we must seek to train men and women who will work in the projects, for unless this is done, and unless there is a pool of qualified applicants for housing positions, there is danger that employees will be chosen for their political contacts rather than for their merits . . .

The future of the housing program and of other federal land activities depends largely on what happens during the coming year. Much will depend on whether the people as well as the administration assume responsibility for the program, lead the fight for its continuance, make it one of their "must" measures. The cooperation of local authorities and a real effort by unofficial groups would do much to bring that about. For among the many measures that come before Congress, with many new issues presented by the present war, with much opinion favoring the limitation of federal operations, the President cannot be expected to press most strongly for measures on which there is only public apathy.

If enough demonstrations can be completed, if enough public interest is stirred to warrant their continuance, housing, rural resettlement and similar measures may reach out of their present place as temporary expedients into something whole, rational, real and permanent. Housing has here been singled out for discussion because space does not permit developing the thesis in the other equally important and related fields in which similar action is necessary and similar techniques must be applied. If confusion or the clamor for economy are allowed to erase the progress so far achieved, it may be years before another similar opportunity presents itself. And in the meantime the situation will continue to deteriorate, for the forces that have brought us to our present position are still the dominant springs of action.

## "Starving on Relief"
**By Keith Hutchison**
**From the** Nation
**February 12, 1936**

*Even though the United States was in the midst of a prolonged economic catastrophe and many of its citizens were suffering greatly and facing dire poverty and hunger, those who were forced to receive relief payments from the federal government in order to survive during the Great Depression felt it was a shameful, humiliating condition. In the days before the Depression, extended families, churches, and private charities would take care of their own and lend them a hand in times of need. Following the stock market crash of 1929 and its long, far-reaching aftermath, however, local communities could no longer offer economic relief to the large numbers of people who needed it.*

*While those who were able-bodied were put to work*
*through the Works Progress Administration (WPA) and other*
*New Deal "workfare" programs, many families had to turn to*
*the government for money that would pay for food and cloth-*
*ing. Even with relief, the poor were sometimes unable to*
*secure the most basic elements required to sustain life. In this*
*selection, Keith Hutchison, a regular contributor to* The Nation
*during the Depression who often examined the progress of*
*the New Deal, reviews the shortcomings of government*
*relief nationwide.*

———◻———

The President is in a fighting mood these days. He trounced
the Tories [conservatives] at Atlanta. He trounced the Tories in
his annual message. He trounced the Tories at the Jackson Day
dinner. Nevertheless, the poor Tories, though trounced, continue
to be well fed. As much cannot be said of the unemployed.

At Atlanta Mr. Roosevelt thought it "of interest to point
out that national surveys prove that the average of our citi-
zenship lives today on what would be called by the medical
fraternity a third-class diet. If the country lived on a second-
class diet we would need to put many more acres than we
use today back into the production of foodstuffs for domestic
consumption. If the nation lived on a first-class diet we
would have to put more acres than we ever cultivated into
the production of an additional supply of things for
Americans to eat. Why, speaking in broad terms in following
up this particular illustration, are we living on a third-class
diet? For the very simple reason that the masses of the
American people have not got the purchasing power to eat

more and better food." Speaking in narrow terms it might also be said that millions of Americans are living on a third-, fourth-, and fifth-class diet because Mr. Roosevelt—for all his Tory-trouncing—insists on cutting relief.

Mr. Roosevelt grew even more eloquent on the subject in his annual message to Congress. "Shall we say," he asked, "to the several millions of unemployed citizens who face the very problem of existence—yes, of getting enough to eat: 'We will withdraw from giving you work, we will turn you back to the charity of your communities and to those men of selfish power who tell you that perhaps they will employ you if the government leaves them strictly alone'?" The answer is that it has now been Mr. Roosevelt's policy for some time to get the federal government out of relief as quickly as possible and in fact to turn "several millions of unemployed citizens who face the very problem of existence—yes, of getting enough to eat"— back on the charity of their communities.

While the President at Atlanta was denouncing "gentlemen in well-warmed and well-stocked clubs" and spreading himself on the subject of third-class diets, relief administrators in the District of Columbia cut families on relief down to a fourth-class diet. An order was issued reducing all relief allowances twenty-five percent. The Washington, D.C., average will now be $22.50 a month per family. At about the same time, too, Secretary [of Agriculture Henry] Wallace was asking in a radio speech, "How can you feed and clothe and maintain the health of a family of four or five properly on $15 or $20 a week?" "The answer," Secretary

Wallace said, "is that you can't." District of Columbia jobless may find it difficult to appreciate the unconscious humor in this or in the fact that in November, when the federal government began to cut relief, a *New York Times* tabulation showed that dividends reached their highest total since June, 1931.

The condition of the unemployed is of little interest to the larger part of the American press. A small group of liberal papers pays some attention to their problems. The Hearst press supplies us with such stories as the recent one published in the *New York American* under the heading, "Give Us More! More! Demand Those on Relief; Mostly Foreigners, Says Bullard." The rest is silence. But from stray items and from the Federated Press, a labor news service, it is possible to put together a picture of the plight of those on the relief rolls.

Here are some glimpses of relief conditions in the country, covering conditions during the past few months:

Allentown, Pennsylvania. Members of the Inter-County Unemployed and Works Division will not dine on turkey Thanksgiving day—or even corned beef; they will be on picket duty all week before local relief offices in Berks, Lehigh, Lancaster, and York counties, protesting against the discontinuance of relief.

Austin, Texas. So many people were thrown off relief last fall "to pick cotton," and never reinstated, that C. E. Wayman, district WPA administrator, complains there are not enough employables left on the rolls to carry on county highway improvements with full man power.

New York City. "Everybody will have a Thanksgiving dinner," the Emergency Relief Bureau announced, but Thanksgiving came and went and everybody didn't. Among those who didn't were the 100,000 human beings represented by 28,000 piled-up relief applications which the bureau's overworked staff has not yet had time to investigate.

Boston (AP). A complaint that payment of a "coolie" wage by the WPA was directly responsible for lowering wage scales of professional and technical workers in and near Boston was made to the state WPA today. A complete investigation was asked, six specific cases being named of alleged "chiseling" among private employers using the WPA wage scale as an excuse for reducing wages.

Phoenix, Arizona. Two more workers have been deported to Mexico as an aftermath of a Phoenix relief workers' strike when police and thugs charged pickets with clubs and tear gas, injuring fifty. The two men, Jose Flores and Jose P. Barcenas, who bring the total number of deportees to seven, were charged with being Communists. Felony charges are still standing against twenty workers who participated in the strike.

Newport, Kentucky (UP). Enraged because they had not been paid, two hundred WPA workers raided a federal relief warehouse here today and seized one hundred bags of flour and other articles before they were dispersed by police.

New Orleans (FP). The tapering-off process preparatory to "quitting this business of relief" is already bearing fruit in New Orleans. Eva Killian, twenty-nine, was declared by physicians to be starving to death when brought by an ambulance to a charity hospital here. She had been living on coffee and bread. A child who fainted at school was found to have been without food for twenty-six hours. A woman and four children were found hiding in an empty house. An aged woman and her fourteen-year-old granddaughter, found rummaging in the scrap heaps behind grocery stores, are but two of hundreds engaged in similar searches.

Chicago (FP). Single men on relief will not have to starve and freeze this winter, the emergency relief commission announces. They will have a chance to enter work camps. "In return for their work they receive sustenance plus one dollar a week in wages," the announcement says.

Newburgh, New York (Special to the *New York Herald Tribune*). About three hundred WPA employees who have received no pay since December fourteen assembled this morning at the City Hall to see what was wrong. They received only about half the pay they expected on December 14.

Vancouver, Washington (FP). A decision that WPA workers are not relief recipients or indigents has been handed down by Washington WPA officials. While at first sight the decision would seem to be in favor of the workers, the real effect of the ruling is to deprive the WPA workers of free medicine, medical aid, and hospital service from the county. The workers are supposed to furnish these items from their meager WPA wages, "just the same as other wage-earners do."

Austin, Texas (FP). Texas relief clients face the prospect of living on half-rations until February. After February there may be no rations at all. County relief administrators have received $375,000 for December, and the state is asking for $500,000 more in federal funds to keep relief up even to its customarily low Southern level. There is little prospect that the added amount will be forthcoming. No provision for the continuance of the state relief system in any form after February was made at the recent legislative session.

Des Moines, Iowa (FP). Calling the $40 a month paid WPA workers in sixty-six of Iowa's ninety-nine counties a "starvation wage," three hundred labor and unemployed delegates, meeting under the chairmanship of President J. C. Lewis of the state federation of labor, called for a statewide strike January 2 for the prevailing scale of wages. The strike would affect nearly thirty thousand workers.

Toledo [Ohio] (FP). The relief crisis is acute in Toledo, as funds appropriated by the state legislature face exhaustion before the middle of the month. Wholesalers have announced they will cut off credit for relief supplies.

Sioux Falls, South Dakota (FP). When South Dakota WPA
workers recently demanded increases in wages which were
frequently lower than direct relief had been, WPA
Administrator M. A. Kennedy issued a statement charging
them with "laziness" and threatening arrests. A week later
he was all smiles and good-will as he announced an average
raise of $8 a month. What changed his tune was that the
Workers' Alliance lined up the trade unions, the Sioux Falls
Ministerial Association, and various civic groups in support
of the jobless, and Kennedy quickly found it possible to get
South Dakota raised from a Class 2 to a Class 1 state, thus
bringing in the higher wage scale.

Boston (FP). Unless the "relief-roll-preferential" system of
hiring is abolished, members of local unions affiliated
with the Boston Building Trades Council will be barred
from transferring from ERA and WPA projects to contract
work. The move is designed to protect the incomes of
building-trades workers not on relief rolls.

St. Louis (FP). WPA workers, already harassed by the difficulties of providing food and clothing for their families on
$55 a month, are facing the prospect of living in the damp
cellars of the city's most run-down buildings. The city's
real-estate exchange, in a move almost tantamount to boycott, has advised its members not to lease property to WPA
workers on the ground that their wages do not permit their
paying rent.

Globe, Arizona (FP). Ten cents a day for food, clothing, and
shelter; this is what Arizona's December allocation of $2,294
for relief in Gila County works out to when divided among
seven hundred persons on the dole. The end of federal relief
is causing untold misery.

And now one last look at what has been going on in
the President's own backyard while he has been trouncing
the Tories:

Washington (FP). With relief cut twenty-five percent on
account of stoppage of federal funds, slow starvation is
already gripping many jobless in the District of Columbia,
case workers report. One relief office has received three letters in a week from clinic doctors who say that relief
patients sent to them don't need medicine, "they need food."

Leroy Halbert, District relief statistician, estimates that of
14,984 persons certified for WPA jobs, 2,500 will receive
less each month on the "security wage" than they have been
getting on direct relief.

## *"The Lasting Values of the WPA"*
### *A Speech by Ellen Woodward*
### *WPA Papers*
### *c. 1935*

As of last May, one in every six persons in the cities, and
one in every eight persons in the rural areas, were
dependent upon public funds for support.

*—Aubrey W. Williams, Assistant Works Progress*
*Administrator (January 15, 1935)*

*Unemployment was a crushing burden on both the economy*
*and social psyche of the United States. Whether laboring in*
*factories, fields, or offices, Americans were an industrious*
*people, and coming off the prosperity of the 1920s, they*
*were used to working. The federal response to the need for*
*jobs was the creation of the Works Progress Administration*
*(WPA) in 1935. This nationwide work-relief program*
*sought to create work for whomever wanted it, from dig-*
*ging ditches, building roads, and working on a farm to*
*writing books and creating art for public spaces. WPA*
*jobs, in addition to giving people much-needed jobs and*
*some money, also created public works of great and endur-*
*ing value to the country. In this circa 1935 speech, Ellen*
*Woodward, the director of the WPA's Women's and*
*Professional Division, argues for the practical and historic*
*importance of this New Deal administration, especially to*
*the nation's unemployed women.*

———□———

No one can better appreciate the lasting values of the work
relief program than we women, for its results affect primarily
that which is closest to our hearts—the home.

Every time a man is taken from the demoralizing ranks
of the jobless, every time a woman is removed from the humiliation of a breadline, and given work to do, a home somewhere becomes more secure.

This, in a word, is the first aim of the Works Progress
Administration: To put destitute people to work at familiar

tasks, that their moral fiber may not be undermined and their hopes and ambitions killed, by the forced acceptance of public charity in the form of a dole.

No one, better than a woman, understands the importance to a Nation of preserving its human resources. The proverb, "What profit it a man that he gain the whole world, if he lose his own soul," may well be paraphrased to read "What profit it a nation to keep its budget balanced if it lose its own life blood—the courage and integrity of its people?"

Obviously, that courage and integrity cannot be fostered on a permanent diet of public dole!

It was with this truth in mind, that President Roosevelt conceived the fundamental idea of a work relief program as an alternative to the dole. It is with this in mind that the Works Progress Administration has labored unceasingly this past year at the titanic task of finding jobs for nearly 4,000,000 of the nation's jobless who were stagnating on relief. How well the aim has been achieved is shown in the latest figures on work relief employment. On March 7th there were over 3,300,000 men and women at work on the entire program, most of them on the 70,000 WPA projects selected.

This job-finding task has been accomplished only by keeping all other considerations secondary to this single aim of finding projects in each community which could be accomplished with the man-power or woman-power available from the relief rolls of the particular community in which they live.

This aim has been stated repeatedly, yet there still remains wide-spread misunderstanding of the basic idea behind WPA and how it operates. And this misunderstanding is responsible for much of the adverse—wholly uninformed—criticism hurled broadside at the WPA.

It is particularly important, it seems to me, for the responsible women of the country to understand, not only the philosophy of the works program, but more specifically the character of the projects designed to give employment to women, for unfortunately, it is this class of project which is receiving some of the most vitriolic and uncalled-for criticism.

Before discussing in detail the projects employing women, I want to emphasize one point. No WPA project in your community or in any other community of the forty-eight states, was planned or selected by administrative officials in Washington, except a very few which are applicable nationally. All other projects are selected, approved and sponsored by local officials or local bodies before they are presented for approval to the State WPA Administrator who in turn submits the proposed project to Washington.

Projects are chosen, as I have indicated, always with the thought uppermost that the specific community has a definite number of specific people to be taken from the relief rolls and put to work, and that they can do this or that type of work.

If your community has no bricklayers or carpenters in need of employment, obviously a construction project requiring much skilled brickwork or carpentry would fail to meet the requirement.

In planning a project to supply jobs for unemployed women, by the same token, the yardstick would scarcely be the needs of the highway or sewerage departments. Widows, school teachers, nurses, and dieticians cannot be put to work digging ditches . . .

Lasting values cannot always be computed in terms of cash. The fact that over 400,000 women have been shifted from relief rolls to jobs has permanent value to the nation, quite aside from the tangible benefits to be reaped from their tasks. Of course the vast majority of these women are heads of families.

Getting back to the program as a whole, who can best judge whether this work is better than the dole, and whether useful and needed work is being done? I submit that the mayors of our cities are more intimately and responsibly concerned with employment and destitution than any other group of public officials in America.

The United States Conference of Mayors recently asked these questions of the chief executives of 100 cities, with a total population of 25 million. The answer, regardless of political creed, was unanimous and emphatic. It was that the people on relief prefer to work for what they get, and that the fruits of this program are of vast and lasting benefit to local communities.

The so-called "white collar projects" of which most of the women's work is a part, comprise less than twenty per cent of the entire 70,000 selected so far, eighty-one per cent, to be exact, of all the projects are construction projects, which include the construction and repair of highways, secondary roads, streets, water and sewerage systems, levees, public buildings, playgrounds and parks.

Not even the most unimaginative man could dispute the "permanent value" of such works as these!

Nor indeed, could he fail to see the value of many of the so-called boondoggles or white collar projects, if he knew what they were all about. There are book-binding projects, for instance, engaging hundreds of persons of both sexes, in the useful task of adding actual dollars and cents to the local and county treasuries by extending the lives of thousands of books in schools and Public Libraries.

In twenty-three states there are projects for the instruction and aid of the blind, the value of which could not begin to be estimated on cost sheets. Women workers predominate on most of these projects, and it is largely the labor of blind or partially blind women who might otherwise have been permanent charges on community relief rolls.

In our work with women, we have a two-fold objective; first, to employ these women on projects according to their skills, and second, to train and retrain them so that through new or increased skills they can earn a livelihood in private employment or run better homes.

More than sixty-five per cent of all the women in this program are at work in sewing rooms, making garments, quilts and other necessary articles for local needy people. The things they produce constitute substantial savings in local Community Chest and other relief budgets, while they themselves are becoming better seamstresses, designers, cutters. They also are trained one hour each day in a wide range of other household arts.

In the hot, school-lunch projects, women who were on relief are earning a living wage cooking and serving hot lunches to undernourished children. Increased school attendance, added weight and better physical condition of the children are immediate results. Already school authorities in some states are planning to carry on this program at the conclusion of WPA.

WPA library projects have established reading rooms in isolated rural areas and city slum sections where books were never before available. Frequently these libraries also have become community work and recreation centers, with fine and able women from the relief rolls providing remarkable leadership.

The quality of this leadership may be judged by a Home Service Center project in Texas. Here a graduate Home Economist, a registered Red Cross nurse, a music conservatory graduate, an expert accountant and others—all women from relief—trained 150 "visiting home aides" to take a weekly lesson on food, health, clothing, and family budgets to mothers of 1,500 underprivileged families.

These nurses concentrate on prevention of communicable diseases, maternity cases, health supervision of infants and school children, examination of tuberculars, child health conferences, immunization clinics . . .

In addition to the fact that needy women have found employment on projects which are improving their training in professional and industrial skills or for the all-important job of homemaker, their service has given 1,900,000 undernourished children of needy families a daily meal on the school lunch program and improved their physical condition. The vast public health nursing program has helped 2,600,000 children. Home visits have reached 3,500,000 homes. Nursing schools have given a better start in life to thousands of tiny tots of preschool age. We recognize the social value of the youth program which has enabled thousands of young people to finish high school and college, and has given thousands of others a chance to put their college training into practical use on some worthwhile project. Nor do we miss the significance of opening up to thousands of illiterate and unschooled, the hitherto unknown world of books, or of projects which are teaching thousands of isolated people to forget toil and hardship and to beat through the shell of shyness and reticence, to learn how to play and sing together in our community recreational centers.

Despite the fact that the needs of specific flesh-and-blood human beings had primary consideration, and projects as such were secondary, hundreds of thousands of miles of roads and streets have been and are being built. Aviation is being spurred by 334 new and improved airports. Great dams, levees, many miles of sewer and drainage systems and five or six thousand public buildings other than schools are on the list. So are thousands of parks, playgrounds and community centers, advances in chemical research, restoration of historic buildings, important archeological discoveries, and location and preservation of valuable historical records.

Every woman has a vital interest in the improvement of school facilities, and in this field, 7,500 projects for school construction or improvement have been approved. I think it is safe to say that there is hardly a county in the United States which is not represented with some school improvement project, from actual new construction to repairs on old buildings and equipment.

These are some of the actual, tangible things which will endure long after the misunderstanding of this program, and we hope, the need for it, have disappeared. The value of this contribution to our well-being is incalculable in dollars and cents.

# CHAPTER FOUR

# CULTURE: OUT OF POVERTY, A CREATIVE FLOWERING

**"Save the Arts Projects"**
**By Elizabeth McCausland**
**From The Nation**
**July 17, 1937**

*By 1937, 70,000 Works Progress Administration (WPA) projects employing skilled and unskilled labor were up and running across the United States. Manual laborers were not the only ones seeking work from the government, however. Tens of thousands of artists—writers, painters, photographers, sculptors, designers, printers—were also left unemployed by the Depression. President Franklin Roosevelt recognized that these artists could be put to work to document the New Deal's effect on individuals and communities throughout the nation as well as provide struggling and downcast Americans with a much-needed uplift in the form of beautiful murals, stimulating plays, and monumental sculptures, all celebrating the strength and resilience of the American spirit. The WPA's Federal Art Project (FAP) was created to achieve these goals. Yet, in the face of widespread hunger and poverty, many politicians and ordinary Americans felt the money spent on arts projects could be put to better use. In this selection, Elizabeth McCausland,*

*an art critic for several Depression-era arts magazines, provides
a spirited defense of the FAP and its contributions to the
rebuilding of a shattered America.*

———□———

The Renaissance lasted three centuries, the Age of Pericles
and the Augustan Age each a half century; for the "cultural
birth of a nation" our government allows less than two years.
With drastic cuts in the Federal Arts Projects effective July
15, the arts in America are on their way back where they
came from, to the status which made necessary the WPA and
white-collar projects.

Yet already the [Federal] Arts Projects have been justified. Since its first performance, February 1, 1936, the Federal
Theater has played to more than twenty-five million, eighty-
seven per cent free and thirteen per cent paid admissions.
From October, 1935, to May 1, 1937, almost sixty million persons have listened to eighty-one thousand performances of
WPA music units, many of them in orphanages, hospitals,
community centers, parks, playgrounds, and churches.
Besides murals, easel paintings, sculptures, and prints allo-
cated to public buildings, the Federal Art Project has reached
the public through its art teaching and through thirty federal
art galleries and art centers established in Tennessee,
Alabama, the Carolinas, Oklahoma, Florida, Utah, Wyoming,
and New Mexico, all in communities where there were none
before. More than a million people visited these centers and
galleries in one year. The Federal Writers Project, handicapped by lack of publishing outlets, has not yet contacted its
widest audience. It is expected, however, that the state guides
will have at least two million circulation.

In "Government Aid During the Depression to Professional, Technical and Other Service Workers," Jacob Baker, assistant to WPA Administrator Harry Hopkins, wrote: "It is only a wide popular participation in artistic activities of any kind that keeps the arts genuinely alive." By this test, the Federal Arts Projects have justified themselves. Nevertheless there has been incessant pressure to reduce expenditures for the arts. Critics argue that to employ forty thousand persons for fourteen months cost the government $46,000,000; and is art worth it? So the cuts continue, because of the Administration's failure to press for adequate appropriations.

In the Federal Theater, employing at the peak more than thirteen thousand, thirty-one per cent of the personnel has been dismissed throughout the country, and Delaware, Rhode Island, Nebraska, and Texas no longer have a theater. This slash is characteristic of what has happened in the drought lands of American culture. Yet it was the hope of the Federal Theater Administration to build a theater belonging to the people. Indeed, it did so; witness the attendance of fourteen thousand children at one federal circus matinee—free. Or take Valley, Nebraska—population one thousand—where eight hundred men, women, and children tried to attend the Federal Theater performance; some had ridden twenty-five and thirty miles to get there. They wrote begging that the company be permitted to settle down there. But the Nebraska unit was wiped out. As regards community drama work, in New York City alone there are over one thousand non-professional groups, attended each week by between twenty-five and thirty-four thousand adults and children, which have given over fifteen hundred plays. All over the United States, in communities so remote and unprivileged that even "the road" had passed them by, this work has gone on.

On the creative side, New York offers outstanding successes, the "Living Newspaper," "Macbeth," "Dr. Faustus," "Murder in the Cathedral," and others, while the simultaneous opening in eighteen cities of twenty-one productions of Sinclair Lewis's anti-fascist "It Can't Happen Here" was a major event in the American theater. In four months it played to two hundred seventy-five persons, grossing $80,000 at an average of 30 cents. "Macbeth," the Negro theater's Shakespeare improvisation, gave one hundred forty-four performances to a total audience of ten thousand, touring four thousand miles, to close at the Texas centennial.

With metropolitan successes have gone important services to the stage, the revival of "the road" through one hundred fifty resident companies in twenty-seven states, the revival of repertory, and the revival—notably in Los Angeles—of stage hits of ten, fifteen, and twenty years ago, such as "Potash and Perlmutter," "The Fool," "Madame X," "The Goose Hangs High," and "Ladies of the Jury," a great aid to students of the evolving American drama. The "Living Newspaper," a montage of cinema, stage, and political rally, is a definite contribution in form.

Of great value, though little advertised, has been the work of the bureaus of research and publication in New York, Los Angeles, Chicago, Birmingham, Seattle, and Oklahoma City, cataloguing, card-indexing, and analyzing every play ever performed or published in the United States. The magazine *Federal Theatre*, published in New York, has tilled a real need of the American people, treating of the theater in human terms. This publication has been discontinued.

So the Federal Theater which brought the living stage to millions of Americans who had never seen a flesh-and-blood actor before—only one high-school pupil out of thirty even in New York City has—faces the future seriously crippled. This, despite the fact that it has won the support of playwrights like George Bernard Shaw and Eugene O'Neill, who offered their plays at extraordinarily low royalties because they believe in a federal theater.

"The salvation of the arts," the Federal Art Project has been called by Lewis Mumford. No less enthusiastic is Ambrose Vollard. The exhibition, "New Horizons in American Art," at the Museum of Modern Art in September, 1936, offered a visual record of the project's first year and won wide critical approval. There were then over five thousand on the FAP's payrolls. Now almost six hundred have been dismissed in New York City alone. Public demand for federal art may be seen in allocations made in New York in 18 months: one hundred thirty-four murals, with eight hundred separate panels; four thousand prints; two thousand nine hundred fifty easel paintings; two hundred four sculptures, including busts, panels, plaques, figures, fountains; two hundred thousand posters for libraries, hospitals, etc.; and the creative photography record, "Changing New York," for the Museum of the City of New York.

The Federal Art Project is notable for art teaching of children centered in New York City, though isolated examples like the work being done in Breathitt County, Kentucky, and in Hawthorne, New York, show what could be done elsewhere.

In New York thirty thousand children attend painting and modeling classes.

The use of art in mental hygiene is only beginning. At Bellevue Hospital in New York City art teaching is used for diagnosis, while at Hawthorne-Cedar Knolls it is used both diagnostically and therapeutically. Both theater and music have also been useful, the Federal Theater giving performances at Bellevue and the Federal Music Project working at the hospital and also at the House of Detention. Such experiments, though unfortunately confined to New York City, point the direction for other communities.

The Index of American Design, set up to record applied arts in our American tradition, ferrets out, collates, and makes accessible source materials in the field of design. The Shaker portfolio, the Pennsylvania German data, and the colored plates already produced in New Mexico of local textiles, hand-carved chests, and folk lore are invaluable. How the projects can be integrated is shown by the Community Playhouse in Albuquerque, New Mexico, where the building was erected by WPA engineers, the drapes woven by WPA women in Colonial Mexican designs, the furniture made by WPA craftsmen after Colonial period furniture, Mexican tin work used for indirect lighting by WPA artisans, and murals of New Mexican scenes painted by WPA artists.

Music for music's sake has been the aim of the Federal Music Project. Founded because of the interpretative musician's plight, its emphasis has been on performance and on teaching, although through the Composers Forum Laboratory new music by contemporary Americans like Roy Harris, Aaron

Copland, Howard Hanson, Roger Sessions, and Virgil Thomson has been given a hearing, while four thousand other compositions by fourteen hundred American composers have been presented. Chiefly the FMP has given music back to the people, as the Federal Theater has given back the living stage. Thus it is not uncommon to hear Brahms wafted by a string quartette from the backyard garden of a settlement house.

An important activity of the project has been recording the folk music of America. Early Mexican, Texas plains and border, Acadian and Creole songs in Louisiana, bayou songs of the Mississippi delta, Kentucky hills folk songs, white and Negro spirituals from the Carolinas, settlers' songs and songs of Indian origin from Oklahoma, early Spanish songs from California, liturgical music from California missions, songs sung by the Penitentes of New Mexico, are a few of the types. Here, too, is aid for those seeking the American tradition.

Music teaching has been carried on by the group method rather than individually. Weekly throughout the United States thirteen hundred teachers have met with two hundred thousand students, aged six to seventy-five. In Mississippi the classes number seventy thousand, in Oklahoma three hundred thousand. Before the Federal Music Project's creation two-thirds of the four million children in one hundred forty-three thousand rural schools were without music instruction. In New York City weekly attendance is sixty thousand; and in nine months prior to April 1, 1937, the total was almost eight million. Participation of the Music Project in National Music Week is another instance of usefulness. Of the thirteen thousand three hundred musicians then on the rolls, eleven thousand took part in New York, Philadelphia, New Orleans, Detroit, California, Mississippi, Minnesota, and Oklahoma. Now this project has had lopped off a fourth of its man-power.

Least favorably situated has been the Federal Writers Project, smallest in numbers employed (about four thousand), and seriously handicapped by lack of outlets for its work. Even so, it has in print or in press thirty-two of the state guides, which are its most ambitious undertaking, a job of writing expected to win at least two million readers in the forty-eight states. The impact of literature is not as easy to evaluate statistically as theater, concert, or gallery attendance. Nevertheless in a window display at project headquarters on East Forty-Second Street, New York City, almost two score titles are shown, including the best seller "Who's Who in the Zoo" and four small magazines published by project workers on their own time and with their own funds. The state guides are a collective adventure in that rediscovery of America which has been going on now for a decade. There are to be separate volumes for each state, Puerto Rico, and the principal cities— in all a total of twenty million words, later to be condensed into six regional guides, the volumes to sell for about $2.00. Washington, DC, and Idaho guides, already published, have won much favorable comment.

Collateral are the survey of federal archives and the historical records survey, which have salvaged valuable public documents. Folk heroes have also been unearthed, such as the New York fireman Mose Humphrey, a worthy companion of Paul Bunyan and John Henry. And a history of the Negro in America has been begun.

Such are the Federal Arts Projects in outline. "One of the gains of the federal work program," wrote Mr. Baker, "has been in its progressive revelation to the American public of the economic significance of cultural activities, which, instead of being luxuries that can be dispensed with, are enrichments of our lives, and material as well as spiritual enrichments." The Roosevelt Administration is dispensing with these enrichments, pleading recovery and economy. Yet in a conference in Washington June 25 with a delegation from New York, Aubrey Williams, assistant WPA administrator, admitted that the only solution of the cultural workers' problem is to establish a permanent arts project, since private industry and private patronage will never absorb these workers. To this end, the unions of the four arts projects are urging a permanent Bureau of Fine Arts, functioning independently under the President. By recognizing the arts' identity of interest and by consolidating administrative duties, pay-roll economies can be accomplished. On the other hand, the economic rights of the worker will be safeguarded, and artist control guaranteed. After the present crisis has been mastered, the next step must be to push this bill.

## From "The Harvest Gypsies"
### By John Steinbeck
### Originally Published in the San Francisco News
### October 1936

*To many, John Steinbeck is the literary voice of the Depression. Born in California in 1902, Steinbeck's first three novels created barely a ripple in the world of literature.*

Tortilla Flat *(1935) marked the turning point in his writing career. Steinbeck built on this success with his poignant study of a migrant family caught in the twin deprivations of the Depression and the Dust Bowl,* The Grapes of Wrath *(1939), which won the Pulitzer Prize.*

*John Steinbeck went on to win the Nobel Prize for Literature in 1962 ". . . for his realistic as well as imaginative writings, distinguished by a sympathetic humor and a keen social perception." Nowhere was his keen social perception more on display than in* The Grapes of Wrath. *"The Harvest Gypsies" is a series of articles on California's migrant workers Steinbeck wrote for the* San Francisco News *(October 5 and 12, 1936) that provided the inspiration and foundation for* The Grapes of Wrath. *The articles later appeared in pamphlet form titled* Their Blood Is Strong *(1938).*

---□---

## Article I

At this season of the year, when California's great crops are coming into harvest, the heavy grapes, the prunes, the apples and lettuce and the rapidly maturing cotton, our highways swarm with the migrant workers, that shifting group of nomadic, poverty-stricken harvesters driven by hunger and the threat of hunger from crop to crop, from harvest to harvest, up and down the state and into Oregon to some extent, and into Washington a little. But it is California which has and needs the majority of these new gypsies. It is a short study of these wanderers that these articles will undertake. There are at least 150,000 homeless migrants wandering up and down the state, and that is an army large enough to make it important to every person in the state.

To the casual traveler on the great highways the movements of the migrants are mysterious if they are seen at all, for suddenly the roads will be filled with open rattletrap cars loaded with children and with dirty bedding, with fire-blackened cooking utensils. The boxcars and gondolas on the railroad lines will be filled with men. And then, just as suddenly, they will have disappeared from the main routes. On side roads and near rivers where there is little travel the squalid, filthy squatters' camp will have been set up, and the orchards will be filled with pickers and cutters and driers.

The unique nature of California agriculture requires that these migrants exist, and requires that they move about. Peaches and grapes, hops and cotton cannot be harvested by a resident population of laborers. For example, a large peach orchard which requires the work of 20 men the year round will need as many as 2000 for the brief time of picking and packing. And if the migration of the 2000 should not occur, if it should be delayed even a week, the crop will rot and be lost.

Thus, in California we find a curious attitude toward a group that makes our agriculture successful. The migrants are needed, and they are hated. Arriving in a district they find the dislike always meted out by the resident to the foreigner, the outlander. This hatred of the stranger occurs in the whole range of human history, from the most primitive village form to our own highly organized industrial farming. The migrants are hated for the following reasons, that they are ignorant and dirty people, that they are carriers of disease, that they increase the necessity for police and the tax bill for schooling in a community, and that if they are allowed to organize they can, simply by refusing to work, wipe out the season's crops. They are never received into a community nor into the life of a community. Wanderers in fact, they are never allowed to feel at home in the communities that demand their services.

Let us see what kind of people they are, where they come from, and the routes of their wanderings. In the past they have been of several races, encouraged to come and often imported as cheap labor; Chinese in the early period, then Filipinos, Japanese and Mexicans. These were foreigners, and as such they were ostracized and segregated and herded about.

If they attempted to organize they were deported or arrested, and having no advocates they were never able to get a hearing for their problems. But in recent years the foreign migrants have begun to organize, and at this danger signal they have been deported in great numbers, for there was a new reservoir from which a great quantity of cheap labor could be obtained.

The drought in the middle west has driven the agricultural populations of Oklahoma, Nebraska and parts of Kansas and Texas westward. Their lands are destroyed and they can never go back to them.

Thousands of them are crossing the borders in ancient rattling automobiles, destitute and hungry and homeless, ready to accept any pay so that they may eat and feed their children. And this is a new thing in migrant labor, for the foreign workers were usually imported without their children and everything that remains of their old life with them.

They arrive in California usually having used up every resource to get here, even to the selling of the poor blankets and utensils and tools on the way to buy gasoline. They arrive bewildered and beaten and usually in a state of semi-starvation, with only one necessity to face immediately, and that is to find work at any wage in order that the family may eat.

And there is only one field in California that can receive them. Ineligible for relief, they must become migratory field workers.

Because the old kind of laborers, Mexicans and Filipinos, are being deported and repatriated very rapidly, while on the other hand the river of dust bowl refugees increases all the time, it is this new kind of migrant that we shall largely consider.

The earlier foreign migrants have invariably been drawn from a peon class. This is not the case with the new migrants.

They are small farmers who have lost their farms, or farm hands who have lived with the family in the old American way. They are men who have worked hard on their own farms and have felt the pride of possessing and living in close touch with the land.

They are resourceful and intelligent Americans who have gone through the hell of the drought, have seen their lands wither and die and the top soil blow away; and this, to a man who has owned his land, is a curious and terrible pain.

And then they have made the crossing and have seen often the death of their children on the way. Their cars have been broken down and been repaired with the ingenuity of the land man.

Often they patched the worn-out tires every few miles. They have weathered the thing, and they can weather much more for their blood is strong.

They are descendants of men who crossed into the middle west, who won their lands by fighting, who cultivated the prairies and stayed with them until they went back to desert.

And because of their tradition and their training, they are not migrants by nature. They are gypsies by force of circumstances.

In their heads, as they move wearily from harvest to harvest, there is one urge and one overwhelming need, to acquire a little land again, and to settle on it and stop their wandering. One has only to go into the squatters' camps where the families live on the ground and have no homes, no beds and no equipment; and one has only to look at the strong purposeful faces, often filled with pain and more often, when they see the corporation-held idle lands, filled with anger, to know that this new race is here to stay and that heed must be taken of it.

It should be understood that with this new race the old methods of repression, of starvation wages, of jailing, beating and intimidation are not going to work; these are American people. Consequently we must meet them with understanding and attempt to work out the problem to their benefit as well as ours.

It is difficult to believe what one large speculative farmer has said, that the success of California agriculture requires that we create and maintain a peon class. For if this is true, then California must depart from the semblance of democratic government that remains here.

The names of the new migrants indicate that they are of English, German and Scandinavian descent. There are Munns, Holbrooks, Hansens, Schmidts.

And they are strangely anachronistic in one way: Having been brought up in the prairies where industrialization never penetrated, they have jumped with no transition from the old agrarian, self-containing farm where nearly everything used was raised or manufactured, to a system of agriculture so industrialized that the man who plants a crop does not often see, let alone harvest, the fruit of his planting, where the migrant has no contact with the growth cycle.

And there is another difference between their old life and the new. They have come from the little farm districts where democracy was not only possible but inevitable, where popular government, whether practiced in the grange, in church organization or in local government, was the responsibility of every man. And they have come into the country where, because of the movement necessary to make a living, they are not allowed any vote whatever, but are rather considered a properly unprivileged class.

Let us see the fields that require the impact of their labor and the districts to which they must travel. As one little boy in a squatters camp said, "When they need us they call us migrants, and when we've picked their crop, we're bums and we got to get out."

There are the vegetable crops of the Imperial Valley, the lettuce, cauliflower, tomatoes, cabbage to be picked and packed, to be hoed and irrigated. There are several crops a year to be harvested, but there is not time distribution sufficient to give the migrants permanent work.

The orange orchards deliver two crops a year, but the picking season is short. Farther north, in Kern County and up the San Joaquin Valley, the migrants are needed for grapes, cotton, pears, melons, beans and peaches.

In the outer valley, near Salinas, Watsonville, and Santa Clara there are lettuce, cauliflowers, artichokes, apples, prunes, apricots. North of San Francisco the produce is of grapes, deciduous fruits and hops. The Sacramento Valley needs masses of migrants for its asparagus, its walnuts, peaches, prunes, etc. These great valleys with their intensive farming make their seasonal demands on migrant labor.

A short time, then, before the actual picking begins, there is the scurrying on the highways, the families in open cars hurrying to the ready crops and hurrying to be first at work. For it has been the habit of the growers associations of the state to provide by importation, twice as much labor as was necessary, so that wages might remain low.

Hence the hurry, for if the migrant is a little late the places may all be filled and he will have taken his trip for nothing. And there are many things that may happen even if he is in time. The crop may be late, or there may occur one of those situations like that at Nipomo last year when twelve hundred workers arrived to pick the pea crop only to find it spoiled by rain.

All resources having been used to get to the field, the migrants could not move on; they stayed and starved until government aid tardily was found for them.

And so they move, frantically, with starvation close behind them. And in this series of articles we shall try to see how they live and what kind of people they are, what their living standard is, what is done for them and to them, and what their problems and needs are. For while California has been successful in its use of migrant labor, it is gradually building a human structure which will certainly change the State, and may, if handled with the inhumanity and stupidity that have characterized the past, destroy the present system of agricultural economics.

## *Article II*

The squatters' camps are located all over California. Let us see what a typical one is like. It is located on the banks of a river, near an irrigation ditch or on a side road where a spring of water is available. From a distance it looks like a city dump, and well it may, for the city dumps are the sources for the material of which it is built. You can see a litter of dirty rags and scrap iron, of houses built of weeds, of flattened cans or of paper. It is only on close approach that it can be seen that these are homes.

Here is a house built by a family who have tried to maintain a neatness. The house is about 10 feet by 10 feet, and it is built completely of corrugated paper. The roof is peaked, the walls are tacked to a wooden frame. The dirt floor is swept clean, and along the irrigation ditch or in the muddy river the wife of the family scrubs clothes without soap and tries to rinse out the mud in muddy water. The spirit of this family is not quite broken, for the children, three of them, still have clothes, and the family possesses three old quilts and a soggy, lumpy mattress. But the money so needed for food cannot be used for soap nor for clothes.

With the first rain the carefully built house will slop down into a brown, pulpy mush; in a few months the clothes will fray off the children's bodies while the lack of nourishing food will subject the whole family to pneumonia when the first cold comes.

Five years ago this family had fifty acres of land and a thousand dollars in the bank. The wife belonged to a sewing circle and the man was a member of the grange. They raised chickens, pigs, pigeons and vegetables and fruit for their own use; and their land produced the tall corn of the middle west. Now they have nothing.

If the husband hits every harvest without delay and works the maximum time, he may make four hundred dollars this year. But if anything happens, if his old car breaks down, if he is late and misses a harvest or two, he will have to feed his whole family on as little as one hundred and fifty.

But there is still pride in this family. Wherever they stop they try to put the children in school. It may be that the children will be in a school for as much as a month before they are moved to another locality.

Here, in the faces of the husband and his wife, you begin to see an expression you will notice on every face; not worry, but absolute terror of the starvation that crowds in against the borders of the camp. This man has tried to make a toilet by digging a hole in the ground near his paper house and surrounding it with an old piece of burlap. But he will only do things like that this year.

He is a newcomer and his spirit and decency and his sense of his own dignity have not been quite wiped out. Next year he will be like his next door neighbor.

This is a family of six; a man, his wife and four children. They live in a tent the color of the ground. Rot has set in on the canvas so that the flaps and the sides hang in tatters and are held together with bits of rusty baling wire. There is one bed in the family and that is a big tick lying on the ground inside the tent.

They have one quilt and a piece of canvas for bedding. The sleeping arrangement is clever. Mother and father lie down together and two children lie between them. Then, heading the other way; the other two children lie, the littler ones. If the mother and father sleep with their legs spread wide, there is room for the legs of the children.

There is more filth here. The tent is full of flies clinging to the apple box that is the dinner table, buzzing about the foul clothes of the children, particularly the baby; who has not been bathed nor cleaned for several days.

This family has been on the road longer than the builder of the paper house. There is no toilet here, but there is a clump of willows nearby where human feces lie exposed to the flies—the same flies that are in the tent.

Two weeks ago there was another child, a four year old boy. For a few weeks they had noticed that he was kind of lackadaisical, that his eyes had been feverish.

They had given him the best place in the bed, between father and mother. But one night he went into convulsions and died, and the next morning the coroner's wagon took him away. It was one step down.

They know pretty well that it was a diet of fresh fruit, beans and little else that caused his death. He had no milk for months. With this death there came a change of mind in his family. The father and mother now feel that paralyzed dullness with which the mind protects itself against too much sorrow and too much pain.

And this father will not be able to make a maximum of four hundred dollars a year any more because he is no longer alert; he isn't quick at piece-work, and he is not able to fight clear of the dullness that has settled on him. His spirit is losing caste rapidly.

The dullness shows in the faces of this family, and in addition there is a sullenness that makes them taciturn. Sometimes they still start the older children off to school, but the ragged little things will not go; they hide in ditches or wander off by themselves until it is time to go back to the tent, because they are scorned in the school.

The better-dressed children shout and jeer, the teachers are quite often impatient with these additions to their duties, and the parents of the "nice" children do not want to have disease carriers in the schools.

The father of this family once had a little grocery store and his family lived in back of it so that even the children could wait on the counter. When the drought set in there was no trade for the store any more.

This is the middle class of the squatters' camp. In a few months this family will slip down to the lower class.

Dignity is all gone, and spirit has turned to sullen anger before it dies . . .

This is the squatters' camp. Some are a little better, some much worse . . . In some of the camps there are as many as three hundred families like these. Some are so far from water that it must be bought at five cents a bucket.

And if these men steal, if there is developing among them a suspicion and hatred of well-dressed, satisfied people, the reason is not to be sought in their origin nor in any tendency to weakness in their character.

## "Americans Go to the Movies"
### By James R. McGovern
### From And a Time for Hope: Americans in the Great Depression
### 2001

> Once I built a railroad, made it run,
> Made it race against time,
> Once I built a railroad, now it's done,
> Brother, can you spare a dime?
> > —"Brother, Can You Spare a Dime?" (1932),
> > lyrics by E. Y. Harburg

*While the Federal Art Project funded the fine arts for the enrichment of America's Depression-ravished soul, the great mass of Americans turned to more commercial entertainment to help them forget their troubles. Commercial radio sent music, comedy, drama, and news directly into American homes, while phonograph records provided listeners with their choice of entertainment. Nightclubs, roadhouses, and theaters saw an explosion of jazz, swing, and big band music. The ten-cent pulp magazines, home to such heroes as Doc Savage and the Shadow, were crowded on newsstands with a large selection of more serious, highbrow magazines. Comic books, birthplace of Superman and Batman, got their start at the height of the Depression. The country was hungry for distraction and fantasy, and in no other way was that hunger better fed than by the more than 5,000 films estimated to have been produced by Hollywood during the 1930s.*

———□———

American movies and radio had one of their most successful decades in the 1930s. Never before were so many Americans in all parts of the country entertained and informed by standardized media. Until then, it was still possible to think of America principally in terms of regions, but by virtue of the impact of national media, national brands, and national advertising, along with improved opportunities for travel, one might, by 1940, think of America as a more unitary culture. Radio and movies not only helped formulate this homogeneity, they also, of course, supplied major clues to its identity with symbolic statements about how Depression Americans felt and what they believed. The fact that the public often sought entertainment from the movies or radio as a mode of escape does not invalidate them as a measure of the national culture. What the American people wished or allowed themselves to escape to was still part of their sensibilities. What played on the dial or on the screen does, in fact furnish important measures of what Americans held dear while in the heart of the Great Depression . . .

The Depression caught Hollywood unprepared and threw it into a panic. Full realization came slowly because box-office receipts held up through 1929 and 1930. By 1931, record losses were recorded at the major studios. Economy measures were adopted, and the price of movie tickets was halved to 25 cents for adults, theater personnel reduced, gimmicks and giveaways were introduced, refreshment stands expanded, and double features became common. Still studio income plummeted in 1933. Proceeds from admissions fell 40% below 1931, a poor year. One trade film journal estimated that 5,000 of the nation's 16,000 theaters had been closed and all major studios were in "desperate trouble." With a mindset shaped by the 1920s, the studios returned to the reliable genre of that period and exaggerated their use. Exotic and bizarre thrillers such as *Freaks* (1932), *Frankenstein* (1932), and *King Kong* (1933) appeared, and especially movies featuring lurid sex and violent crime became staples of the movie studios. Far from being a golden age of films, the studios chose cheap and sensational subjects and themes and imposed them on the public, hoping these time-tested formulas would draw large audiences once again and offset losses from the Depression.

Gangster films had special appeal for Hollywood in the early 1930s because they were economical to produce, very exciting, and reflected an America awash with crime. Statistics compiled by the federal government showed a constant rise in the crime rate from 6.8 homicides per 100,000 people in 1920 to 9.7 in 1933, a 30% increase and a peak for homicides in the 1930s. Prohibition contributed significantly to the dramatic rise in crime and homicides. Since organized crime usually carried out its operations on an interstate basis, state police were powerless to act, while the federal government's authority in interstate crime enforcement was then restricted to intercepting traffic in stolen cars. American movie audiences were interested in gangsters too because they were tough and exciting and could deal with difficulties, but also, one suspects, because they feared them as people who were turning their world upside down. All these considerations explained why *Little Caesar* (1930), featuring Edward G. Robinson, and *Public Enemy* (1931), with Jimmy Cagney (both stars of unusual personal magnetism), were popular and nominated for awards.

Surely, neither gave comfort or hope about the human condition at a time of deepening depression. Rico Bandello (Robinson), as "Little Casear," with an obsessive desire "to be somebody," has a terrible sense of inferiority that he compensated for by ruthless killing. He rises to the top of his gang because he is not afraid to kill, unlike mobsters who have grown soft. He also regards discretion and interest in women as signs of weakness. Rico finally shoots the police commissioner and then a member of his own gang on the steps of the church where the gangster had gone to confess his wrongdoings. Rico himself is later gunned down by the police. It is hard to credit him with more than a perverse application of Horatio Alger; he is truly a study in "social pathos" . . .

In 1934, Hollywood began to shed its preoccupation with the destructive and outlandish with the issue of the remarkable screwball comedy *It Happened One Night*, starring Claudette Colbert and Clark Gable and directed by the prophetic Frank Capra. By 1935, the changeover had become virtually complete; the studios had come full circle and were featuring positive interpretations of American life and applauding the nation's institutions, traditions, and opportunities. Three major factors were responsible: the New Deal stabilized American society by achieving centralization of authority and projecting a caring and benevolent sense of national community; there were also increasingly negative responses by the public to the ideology of the movies. Audiences objected to their antisocial character and their criticism of institutions and traditional values. Prominent Catholic laity and clerics would spearhead this reaction, but it is a mistake to assume that concern about these issues was restricted to Catholics. The third major factor was that movie revenues began to climb. Once the new focus for films was adopted by the major studios, Hollywood found what it was desperately searching for—a formula to prosper in the Depression.

In essence, the New Deal restored a basic order to American life by performing important, integrative functions. This is apparent in its impact on the cinema. By sponsoring the Twenty-first Amendment to abolish Prohibition, the New Deal dealt a lethal blow to crime and its secretive networks. It is estimated that one-third of the homicides in America in 1933 were linked to criminal vendettas by persons violating Prohibition. Now with a stroke of the pen, this species of mayhem largely disappeared. This, together with expansion of the federal government's prerogatives in interstate crime and the emergence of a prestigious Federal Bureau of Investigation (FBI), took the gangsters off the streets. Criminals who held out were rigorously pursued and each victorious outcome by federal agents became a parable for a resurgent community spirit; good and effective men wore federal insignia and big-time criminals were finally paying the wages of sin.

The impact of these developments registered quickly in Hollywood's "crime movies." Their turnaround is underscored by the fact that the new heroes, now police and FBI, were the former film gangsters, Jimmy Cagney and Edward G. Robinson, while the former crime movies became law-and-order movies. Jimmy Cagney in *G-Man* (1935) comes out of a shady past, keeping alive the basis of his persona in *Public Enemy*, but with a clear change in character and a strong preference for preserving community against irresponsible individualism. Although nearly dismissed from the FBI because of his former gangland connections, he vindicates the bureau's confidence by avenging the death of a fellow-G-man. Viewers of the film are exposed in the interim to imposing displays of the FBI's power and efficiency—its crime labs, fingerprinting collections, tough physical training, and competent agents. Everyone was impressed. One character who supplies information to the FBI in the film concedes he did so because he didn't want to get into trouble with its agents. A theater owner in Washington, DC, found record audiences attending *G-Man* over a July 4th weekend in 1935. Another in Lamar, Missouri, wrote about *G-Man* "We honestly believe that every theatre should play this for the reason it leaves a lot of people thinking our government is OK." *G-Man* played fifty days in New York and Los Angeles, eight more than *Little Caesar* or *Public Enemy*. The new surge of anti-crime movies cast Edward G. Robinson as an FBI agent. In *Bullets or Ballots*, he insinuates himself into a gang and destroys it, thus becoming an antithesis of Rico. Law enforcement even came to be invested with an aura of patriotism. *Special Agent* (1935) opened with a picture of the American flag

followed by a speech overheard from the Senate Building laud-
ing the FBI for taking steps to rid the country of criminal elements. There is reason to believe that the public that attended
these films felt more secure and hopeful because, in fact as well
as film, America's basic institutions were working . . .

It is appropriate to describe the great period in the history
of movies from 1935 to 1939 as Hollywood's "Golden Age." Its
stars were smooth and often sophisticated; its dancing in the
form of Ginger Rogers and Fred Astaire classic gracefulness; its
film subjects and treatments generally elevating to the spirit; its
directors exceptionally talented; and its popularity then at an all-
time zenith. Robert Sklar sees this period as one in which film
producers first became fully aware of the power of their medium
and consciously crafted an affirmative view of American life to
buoy the jaded spirits of depressed Americans. From the standpoint of social history, it would seem correct instead to credit the
American people for diverting the moguls from purely market
considerations to a course that acknowledged the importance of
their social values and historical traditions. Hollywood's role in
the late 1930s was less one of initiative and myth-making than
one of reinforcing public preferences and commitments. This
explains that assortment of popular films issued in Hollywood's
Golden Age that celebrate small towns and their responsible
political representatives, the importance of home and family,
neighborliness and generosity, love's ability to conquer class
interest, the special place of America in the world, and, of
course, the idea that "tomorrow, after all, is another day." . . .

Film as an instrument of popular culture dramatically
changed course after 1935 and became an apologist for the
American way of life. It would almost seem that two such dia-

metrically opposed spirits in film, one from 1930 to 1934, the other from 1935 to 1939, could not inhere in a single decade. In the earlier period, the movie industry panicked over declining revenues and chose for its staples violence, sexual license, and flamboyant individualism, familiar successful themes from the 1920s. Unwittingly, it imposed an unacceptable ideology for the depression decade. The displeasure of movie patrons became increasingly acute—the extreme individualism and nonconformity advanced by film jeopardized public reliance on family, religion, and community that many regarded as essential for dealing with the era's uncertainties. The movies also seemed to champion lawlessness and harpoon government that supplied indispensable services. Besides, there was fear that the movies were fostering negative views about America's ability to cope with problems such as crime and perhaps its unique ability to transcend limits that history imposed on other countries. After public protest, movies in the mid- and late 1930s made restitution. They played to banner sized movie audiences, and they helped strengthen the social system in ways that Americans cherished. Popular culture in the term of movies then became still another instrument to help them cope with the depression's vicissitudes.

## "Keeping an Eye on America: The Contradictions of Depression-Era Photography"
### By Giovanna Dell'Orto
### From the Minnesota Daily
### 1998

*It might seem strange that the federal government would expend funds on a photographic record of rural America while many of its citizens starved, but the Farm Security Administration (FSA) believed that by documenting American poverty, it was helping address the needs of the poor. The objective of the FSA was to inform people, through pictures, about the enormous human problem with which the Farm Security Administration was struggling. It hoped that the photographs would make better-off Americans more sympathetic to the plight of the poorest citizens, most of them farmers, and inspire them to help out in any way they could, not least of all by continuing to support President Franklin Roosevelt's New Deal.*

*Photographer Walker Evans and writer James Agee were two of the FSA's most talented workers. They collaborated on a* Fortune *magazine article (which became a book called* Let Us Now Praise Famous Men*) about sharecroppers in the Deep South. They were joined in their FSA efforts by other noted photographers, including Dorothea Lange and Ben Shahn. All of these FSA artists struggled with the competing demands of art photography on the one hand and socially minded, unvarnished documentary on the other, of a respect for human dignity and privacy weighed against the imperatives of the probing eye of journalism. The following selection is a review of a 1998 art exhibit of Depression-era photography at the Weisman Art Museum in Minneapolis, Minnesota. The author, Giovanna Dell'Orto, is a journalist for the* Minnesota Daily.

———■———

*It seems to me curious, not to say obscene and thoroughly terrifying . . . to pry intimately into the lives of an undefended*

*and appallingly damaged group of human beings, an ignorant*
*and helpless rural family, for the purpose of parading the*
*nakedness, disadvantage and humiliation of these lives before*
*another group of human beings, in the name of science, of*
*honest journalism.*

—*James Agee,* Fortune

In 1936, when photographers James Agee and Walker Evans
were reporting on tenant farmers in Alabama for *Fortune* magazine, Agee expressed his moral discomfort toward the documentary genre with these bitter words. He felt challenged by
the endemic paradoxes of documentary art: its tensions
between the objective and the posed, the dual search for reality
and aesthetic success, the goal of arousing the audience's
sympathy and the fear of catering to its morbid fascinations
with suffering.

  Other artists engaged in the New Deal's vast photographic
project, from Dorothea Lange to Ben Shahn, walked the same
fine line, and *The Documentary Eye*, the Weisman's small but
poignant photographic exhibition, presents these concerns to
the viewer's eye with both beauty and consciousness.

  The emotional impact of Floyd Burroughs' direct gaze,
the painful determination in his eyes and the weary frown
on his brow, might be significantly less draining to a contemporary audience than it was to Evans when he portrayed
this young cotton sharecropper. Like the best examples of
photojournalism, these pictures are so visually acute that
their social content risks being overshadowed. Especially

today, firmly ensconced in the American collective mind as Depression-era icons, most of the exhibited photographs may cultivate only a purely aesthetic interest.

Lange's classically balanced composition of a black couple laboring in a Georgia field—their tall, intersecting hoes silhouetted against a low, uninterrupted horizon—resonates with powerful geometry. Marion Post Wolcott's blond toddler caressed by sunlight, picking cotton blooms among plants taller than he is, displays virtuoso lighting effects. But to their creators and their intended audience, these images carried a very explicit and urgent sociopolitical message.

The institution of the gigantic Farm Security Administration photography project was a crucial component of Roosevelt's efforts to resuscitate the American economy (and particularly the struggling agricultural sub-culture of the South). Renowned artists and young unknowns alike were put on the government's payroll and assigned to provide their coordinator, the economist Roy Stricker, with thousands of negatives and prints of the poverty threatening rural America. Simply put, they were intended to sell New Deal policies to both Congress and its constituency, middle-class America, through a well-orchestrated mass distribution of newly popular photo magazines.

Although this agenda determined the usage of pictures, the photographers strove for a certain degree of autonomy. Some images capitulate to blatant propaganda, like Russell Lee's "A magazine rack in the home of a family who will benefit by the FSA Resettlement Project, Louisiana," a double advertisement for the politician and the media businessman.

But excessive modern skepticism might be anachronistic here. Just like Agee, most of the artists felt revulsion at their own intrusiveness, but realized their responsibility to establish a connection with the more prosperous side of America and incite it to help heal the crisis. Although influenced by different backgrounds and political preferences, they believed in informing the public—and doing so without compromising the integrity of their subjects.

"You have more or less of a snapshot of reality, from completely candid to utterly staged," says Paula Rabinowitz, professor of English and American Studies. Rabinowitz, who is writing a book on the subject, does not equate this politicized branch of documentary art with exploitation of its subject, as critics have often branded New Deal photography. She envisions the act of documentation as an exchange between portrayer and portrayed.

It is impossible to face these photographs today without feeling the uneasiness of the genre's contradictions—immediacy tamed by the very distance of the medium, the beauty of the subjects' tragedy, the camera's mechanical intimacy, the predetermined script of the dignity of labor and the moderate suggestion of racial integration. Images of mothers in rags and barefoot children with precociously blank stares or unsuspecting smiles mythologize the suffering of rural society's most sacred tenet: the matriarchal family, itself a symbol of fecundity. But the photographs sincerely sympathize with this fragment of society left behind in the national race for progress.

In some pictures, the contrast between America's two faces becomes starkly literal. In Arthur Rothstein's "Negro

Girl, Gee's Bend, Alabama," a black girl stands at the window of her sod-and-logs shack, staring past a shutter made of old newspapers that feature a smiling, domestic blonde.

Often, though, the issue of race receives a more ambiguous treatment. A photograph of a devastated plantation house, crumbling with the eerie shabbiness of a ghost mansion and described as "now occupied by Negroes," buys into the stereotype of the ruin brought to southern society by integration. Most images of African-Americans, however, strive to convey a reassuring sense of peaceful optimism. Both Lee and Lange portray black workers in contented attitudes of rest, with expressions of either heroic endurance or smiling good mood.

Rothstein's "Wife and Children of a Negro Sharecropper, Tupelo, MS" is one of the most intimate, spontaneous images in the exhibition. Its close-up image focuses on a beautiful young mother who's playfully looking off over her left shoulder, smiling at a joke and holding an infant whose head is still turned backward toward home.

But the most extreme image about racial relationships belongs to Carl Mydans. A couple walks confidently along a dusty road, carrying the few bundles that likely contain their every possession. As the title explains, they are moving away in search of better-paying jobs—the very icon of the displaced worker striving toward new horizons, except for the fact that he is black and she is white. Anyone who has ever read Faulkner can perceive the radical quality of such integration, since southern customs at the time cringed in terror at the mention of miscegenation.

In fact, reducing these images to mere historical documents might be precocious even in the seemingly prosperous 1990s. Documentary art and socially involved art, along with their paradoxes, have not vanished in the reflexively apathetic and superficially trivial contemporary political arenas.

If you drive about one hour south of Memphis on rural Highway 61, deep into the immense cotton fields of Mississippi, you might find that the downtrodden world of New Deal photographs was not merely a propaganda tool. Under the constant buzzing of cicadas, rows of shacks line the fields and people still squat under their patched-up porches watching the rarefied traffic and sharing laughter with their neighbors. Even today, the scene in Mydans' photograph seems unlikely here.

Both the contemporary viewer and the Depression photographer must reconcile what are often grim surroundings with their aesthetic standard. Agee and Evans describe the contradictions in documentary by saying:

If complications arise, that is because [we] are trying to deal with it not as journalists, sociologists, politicians, entertainers, humanitarians, priests, or artists, but seriously.

For all its pitfalls, the serious documentary eye has not stopped looking—and should not stop.

# CHAPTER FIVE

# TIME, CONTINUITY, AND CHANGE: REBIRTH OF A NATION, DEATH OF A SOLDIER

### "What We Are Fighting For"
### By Eleanor Roosevelt
### From American Magazine
### July 1942

*In an age when a First Lady's duties included hosting White House teas and christening ships for the newsreel cameras, Eleanor Roosevelt, wife of President Franklin Roosevelt, defied expectations. She shared FDR's political beliefs and was his working partner in all of his campaigns and public service endeavors. Indeed, with her husband often confined to a wheelchair in later life due to the effects of polio, Eleanor became his eyes and ears, going where he could not.*

*Eleanor Roosevelt traveled America, fighting tirelessly for the betterment of all its citizens. She gave lectures and radio broadcasts and wrote a daily syndicated newspaper column, all of which supported her humanitarian efforts. If anyone could speak out on the moral justifications for America's entry into World War II, it was she. Eleanor's reasons for supporting American involvement in the war, despite the nation's lingering exhaustion at the tail end of*

*the Depression, are based in large part upon her desire to*
*create a nation and a world in which the humiliations of*
*poverty, need, and powerlessness will never again have to*
*be experienced by a single individual, regardless of race,*
*creed, or class.*

——□——

A young officer said to me the other day, "If I asked my men
why they are fighting, the answer probably would be, 'Because
those are our orders.'"

A great many people think in much the same terms—in
fact, the great mass of people in our country, if asked why
they are fighting, would answer, "Because we have to."

No great conviction seems to have come as yet to the
people of the nation to make them feel that they fight for
something so precious that any price is worth paying.

To me, it seems we fight for two things. First, for freedom.
Under that we list:

• Freedom to live under the government of our choice.

• Freedom from economic want.

• Freedom from racial and religious discrimination.

Second, for a permanent basis for peace in the world. Under
this we list:

• A world economy guaranteeing to all people free trade
  and access to raw materials.

• A recognition of the rights and the dignity of the
  individual.

- Machinery through which international difficulties may be settled without recourse to war. This necessitates international machinery as well as an international police force.

Gradually our people have accepted the fact that we are fighting for freedom, but I am constantly told that they are not really conscious of what freedom has been lost or endangered. They still feel safe. War is still remote, save for the families who have men in the Armed Forces. The individual civilian's place in this war is still not well defined.

Groups of people, especially young people, talk a great deal about post-war aims. They say the war is worth fighting only if, by fighting it, we are going to create a brave new world. But what kind of a new world?

We'd better be fairly sure of the kind of new world we want. When we look over the past few years, we discover that the war, as we know it now, is only a phase of something which has been going on ever since the last war—a kind of world revolution. It is a worldwide uprising by the people which manifested itself first in those countries where the pressure was greatest. It is a determination to accept whatever offered the promise of giving them and their families, their parents and their children, a better way of life . . .

Today we in the United States find ourselves a nation involved in this revolution, and the war is only its outward and visible sign. We are a part, our people are a part, of a worldwide desire for something better than has been had heretofore.

The same seeds have been germinating here that germinated and burst through the ground in Russia, Germany, Italy, Spain, and France. That they were still only germinating in Great Britain and in the United States when the war began is because we have been a little better off and have had people among us with sufficient wisdom to recognize some of the aspirations of human beings and to try to meet them. However, neither in Great Britain nor in the United States were they really being fully met.

Time and again I have heard the claim: "But what we have had has been good. Oh, to be sure, during the Depression some of our people were hungry, some of our people went without shelter and clothing, but look at what we did for them! Our government began to feed them. We provided them with work which, though not very remunerative, kept them alive. Then they always had the hope that things would be better. We might get back to those good old days of the 20s, when all but some five million people actually had jobs, and some people really had more material things than they knew what to do with." But we were not getting back to "those good old days" as quickly as some people hoped. The five million had been added to, and there was a question in a great many people's minds whether the good old days were good enough for the vast majority of people.

I think most of us will agree that we cannot and do not want to go back to the economy of chance—the inequalities of the 20s. At the end of that period we entered an era of social and economic readjustment. The change in our society came about through the needs and the will of society. Democracy, in its truest sense, began to be fulfilled. We are fighting today to continue this democratic process. Before the war came, all the peoples of the world were striving for the same thing, in one way or another. Only if we recognize this general rising of the peoples of the world can we understand the real reason why we are in the war into which we were precipitated by the Japanese attack. Only if we realize that we in the United States are part of the world struggle of ordinary people for a better way of life can we understand the basic errors in the thinking of the America First people.

A few short months ago the America First people were saying that they would defend their own country, but that there was no menace to this country in the war going on in Europe and Asia. Why could we not stay within our own borders and leave the rest of the world to fight out its difficulties and reap the benefit ourselves of being strong from the material standpoint when others were exhausted? We would make money out of other nations. We would lose nothing, we would only gain materially, and we would be safe. Why stick our necks out? This sounded like an attractive picture to many people, but unfortunately it wasn't a true one.

One phase of the world revolt from which we could not escape concerns something which people do not like to talk about very much—namely, our attitude toward other races of the world. Perhaps one of the things we cannot have any longer is what Kipling called "The White Man's Burden." The other races of the world may be becoming conscious of the fact that they wish to carry their own burdens. The job which the white race may have had to carry alone in the past, may become a cooperative job.

One of the major results of this revolution may be a general acceptance of the fact that all people, regardless of race, creed, or color, rate as individual human beings. They have a right to develop, to carry the burdens which they are capable of carrying, and to enjoy such economic, spiritual, and mental growth as they can achieve.

In this connection, a problem which we Americans face now at home is the activity of the Japanese and Germans in sowing seeds of dissension among the ten percent of our population comprising the Negro race. The Negroes have been loyal Americans ever since they were brought here as slaves. They have worked here and they have fought for our country, and our country fought a bloody war to make them citizens and to insist that we remain a united nation.

They have really had equality only in name, however. Therefore, they are fertile ground for the seeds of dissension. They want a better life, an equality of opportunity, a chance to be treated like the rest of us before the law. They want a chance to hold jobs according to their ability, and not to be paid less because their skins are black. They want an equal break with the men and women whose skins happen to be white.

They must have a sense of economic equality, because without it their children cannot profit by equal education. Moreover, how can they have equal education if they haven't enough to eat, or if their home surroundings are such that they automatically sink to the level of the beasts? They must have, too, a sense that in living in a Democracy, they have the same opportunity to express themselves through their government and the same opportunity as other citizens for representation. They aspire to the same things as the yellow and brown races of the world. They want recognition of themselves as human beings, equal to the other human beings of the world.

Of course, they are a part of this revolution—a very active part because they have so much to gain and so little to lose. Their aspirations, like those of other races seeking recognition and rights as human beings, are among the things we are fighting for. This revolution will, I think, establish that the human beings of the world, regardless of race or creed or color, are to be looked upon with respect and treated as equals. We may prefer our white brothers, but we will not look down on yellow, black, or brown people.

Another of our aims undoubtedly is to assure that among our natural resources manpower is recognized as our real wealth. No future economic system will be satisfactory which does not give every man and woman who desires to work, an opportunity to work. Our people want to be able to earn, according to their abilities, not only what this genera-tion considers the decencies of life, but whatever else they can gain by their labors. Standards of living may vary with the years, but we must see to it that all our men and women have the opportunity to meet them. The world we live in will not be the same after this war is over, but no one who travels through the length and breadth of the country will believe we need accept a low standard of living. We are still an undevel-oped country. We still have untold natural resources. All we have to do is to face the fact that real wealth lies in the resources of a country and in the ability of its people to work. You may lose everything you have put away in the safe-deposit box, but if you can work and produce with your hands or with your head, you will have wealth. For the wealth of a people lies in the land and in its people and not in the gold buried somewhere in vaults!

The economists can work out the details of our adjustments, but, in a broad way, this war will establish certain economic procedures. We will no longer cling to any type of economic system which leaves any human beings who are willing to work, without food and shelter and an opportunity for development. The people themselves are going to run their own affairs; they are not going to delegate them to a few people and become slaves to those few. Having established that, we will still be carrying out the revolution, the revolution of people all over the world.

Lastly, we are fighting, along with many other people, in other countries, for a method of world cooperation which will not force us to kill each other whenever we face new situations. From time to time we may have other world revolutions, but it is stupid that they should bring about wars in which our populations will increasingly be destroyed. If we destroy human beings fast enough, we destroy civilization. For many years after the war we will be finding ways to accomplish things which the people want to accomplish without destroying human beings in battle. We must set up some machinery, a police force, even an international court, but there must be a way by which nations can work out their difficulties peacefully.

The totalitarian way of revolution being abhorrent to us, we, in the United States, are dedicating all we have to the revolution which will make it possible for us to go forward in the ways of freedom. We cannot stand still for the pleasure of a few of our citizens who may grow weary of the forward march. We accept the will of the majority of our citizens. We fight this war in about the same spirit in which our first Revolution was carried on. We will have to part with many things we enjoy, but if we determine to preserve real values, the essentials of decent living for the people as a whole, and give up trying to keep them in the hands of a few, we will win the war in the democratic way. The ways of Fascism and Nazism will be defeated and the way of democracy will triumph.

Most of our present-day ideals were present in the last war twenty-five years ago. President Wilson's Fourteen Points really dealt with these same questions. The men who fought the war to end war—the war to establish democracy—were not as realistic as we are today, however. They had not been tried as we have been tried in the past few years. They had never been obliged to define the specific things for which they fought. Most of us today who have a clear picture of what we think is happening in the world are sure of the objectives for which we are going to sacrifice, but we are not willing to sacrifice for anything less than the attainment of these objectives.

Once the people as a whole understand that these are the objectives of the leaders of the United Nations, there will be sorrow at the young lives that are being sacrificed, but not bitterness. All will be willing to accept civilian hardships and sacrifice, for there will be full understanding that failure to win the revolution in the way of democracy would bring only unbearable disaster.

The war is but a step in the revolution. After the war we must come to the realization of the things for which we have fought—the dream of a new world.

## "The Tractor Revolution"
**By James H. Street**
**From the Atlantic Monthly**
**June 1946**

*Many in the United States were too busy fighting World War II to notice that wartime production had lifted the country out of the Great Depression. The vast war machine needed uncountable tons of goods and products to be produced in order to keep the troops clothed, fed, and armed. Everything from weapons and vehicles to uniforms and foodstuffs had to be produced quickly and in great quantity.*

*When the war ended in 1945, America was facing its brightest future in more than fifteen years. It was now a dominant superpower, its economy was booming, and its citizens were more optimistic than they had been since before the crash of 1929. On farms once blighted by dust and a devastated economy, the humble tractor seemed to be emerging as the hero of the new economy, leading to an explosion in agricultural production and efficiency. Not everyone felt American agriculture was again on solid ground, however, or would never again experience a catastrophe like that of the Dust Bowl and Depression. James H. Street, an agricultural economist with the Department of Agriculture, sounded a few warning notes in a 1948* Atlantic Monthly *article about the dangers posed to American farmers and the economy by agricultural mechanization.*

——□——

During the war years, our American farmers achieved the most remarkable crop-production record of all time. In 1942 they raised more food than in any previous year, and by the peak year of 1944 their production exceeded the 1935–1939 average by 36 per cent.

This enormous increase in production is the more extraordinary because it was accomplished in the face of a decline of about two and a half million in the farm labor force from 1940 to 1944. Farmers of course worked longer hours during the war, and they were aided by generally favorable weather. But by far the most significant reason for their increased productivity has been the sweeping technological change in agriculture.

Despite wartime restrictions on the manufacture of farm machinery, the number of tractors on American farms has increased by over 34 per cent since 1940. There have likewise been amazing increases in the use of highly specialized tilling and harvesting equipment. During the first three years of the war alone the number of mechanical corn-pickers increased by 29 per cent, combine harvesters by 31 per cent, pickup hay-balers by 67 per cent, and milking machines by 49 per cent. In 1943 one third of the entire United States corn crop was harvested by machine, although the corn-picker had been introduced only a few years before.

The trend toward industrialization means better agriculture, but it threatens to disrupt our entire mode of rural life. Almost until the present generation, the average farmer's aspiration was to own just enough land to support his family comfortably according to modest rural standards. It was a subsistence-based concept of agriculture, with the emphasis on production for use rather than for sale. The family-sized, fully owned farm has remained the American ideal, but in recent years many a farmer has struggled up the successive rungs of the ladder, from wage work to sharecropping to cash tenancy to encumbered ownership, only to discover that a neighbor who is merely renting or managing land is better off than he with his heavy debt load. Moreover, the definition of a family-sized farm is now more commonly set by the productive capacity of a man's tractor than by the needs of his family.

An Army poll taken before demobilization began indicated that from 800,000 to 1,000,000 servicemen intended to go into full-time farming after their discharge. Another 500,000 planned to take up part-time farming. These prospective farmers, together with thousands of industrial workers who left the farms temporarily during the war and additional thousands of farmers' sons maturing each year, will undoubtedly enter into heavy competition for farm land. Land values in some areas are already inflated, and agricultural officials fear a land boom similar to the one which resulted in so many farming failures after the First World War.

Although many people still identify the soil with personal security, and every depression has seen a drift "back to the land," the long-range movement is toward the city and town.

The proportion of the American working population engaged in agriculture was only 26 per cent in 1929, and by 1943 it had dropped to about 15 per cent. Of the estimated 6,300,000 persons who left the farms from 1940 to 1944, it is likely that a majority will never be able to return to an adequate livelihood in farming . . .

The gasoline tractor, though by no means the first important invention in agriculture's technological revolution, was perhaps the most dramatic. Its greater pulling power vastly increased the effectiveness of large implements like the harvester-thresher combine. During World War I the tractor and combine began to turn the Great Plains into a grain factory of previously unimagined proportions. The number of man-hours required to grow an acre of wheat dropped sharply, and the size of individual farms could be expanded. Many returning soldiers of that war found they were no longer needed on the farm, and were forced to join the unemployment ranks of 1921.

The mechanization of wheat farming went on long after the war. Between 1926 and 1930, implement manufacturers in this country turned out 115,000 combines, as compared with 25,000 during the previous five years. By 1938, 90 per cent of the wheat in Kansas was being harvested by combine.

Many who read *The Grapes of Wrath* toward the close of the Depression were startled to learn what had been going on in the rural areas of the country. Some wondered whether the large population movements which Steinbeck described could actually have taken place. But not the families who

experienced those hungry years in the Southwest. During
the period from 1930 to 1938, over 60,000 tractors came
into Texas alone—an increase of 165 per cent over the number
already in use. C. Horace Hamilton, rural life economist at
Texas Agricultural and Mechanical College, who has made
an intensive study of the human consequences of agricultural
mechanization, estimated conservatively that each new tractor
meant at least one family displaced from the land. He cited
one instance in which as many as nine families were displaced by a single tractor.

The Okies did not come from Oklahoma alone. They came
from the corn and wheat areas as well as the cotton lands.
They came from fruit and vegetable farms scattered from New
Jersey to Florida. They came even out of the Ozarks and the
Appalachians, those last strongholds of subsistence farming.
Large numbers of these workers have been temporarily
anchored by industrial jobs or military service; but if industrial
employment falls off, they will soon be on the move again,
looking for jobs and farms in the rural areas they know best.

The number of tractors on United States farms was
nearly doubled during the ten years before the war; by 1940
there were about 1,600,000 in use. When you consider that
those were largely depression years and that the purchase of
a tractor and complementary equipment is one of the major
undertakings of a lifetime for the average farmer, you realize
that something was literally shoving farmers along the road
to mechanization. If they could not buy on the installment
plan, they often mortgaged their farms to acquire machines
during this period.

There are now well over 2,000,000 tractors on American farms, and they have had a powerful influence on the consolidation of landholdings. The use of power-drawn equipment usually means the need for a larger farm, both because it is easier to work more land and because the larger investment requires a larger return. Farm operators ordinarily solve the problem by buying or renting additional acreage, which frequently means the displacement of the previous tenants. The Corn Belt farmer who used to think that a quarter section was all a man could reasonably handle may now feel cramped unless he can operate a section or more. Not uncommonly his holdings are scattered in tracts several miles apart; the problem of distance has become less important with the use of the farm truck and the rubber-tired tractor . . .

The farmers who were displaced by consolidation have inevitably entered into competition with each other for the limited remaining acreage. As a result the number of very small farms has been increasing at the same time that large farms have been multiplying. Census figures do not always make clear that these subdivided farms are on the poorer lands, or that they represent the tightening confines of America's rural slums.

It is thus paradoxical that the tendency toward greater commercialization on the part of some farmers drives other farmers to an increasing dependence upon subsistence farming. In ordinary times the competition in the limited agricultural market is so severe that only the low-cost producers can afford to stay in business. The rest are forced to live on what they raise, rather than what they sell. Analysis of census figures by the Bureau of Agricultural Economics has shown that the overwhelming bulk of the agricultural production which goes into commercial channels is produced by less than half of the nation's farms. In 1939, one third of the farms in the United States marketed only 3 per cent of all farm products sold, and another third produced only 13 per cent additional of the total marketings.

If markets shrink again during the next few years, it will be the small, less efficient producer who is squeezed out of the commercial economy and perhaps out of farming entirely. This result may be better for agriculture as a whole, but it leaves unsolved the problems of those who must find their livelihood elsewhere . . .

The future of American agriculture poses a major problem for national policy. As with all social problems of this magnitude, no simple solution is possible, and only a few suggestions can be sketched here . . .

On the positive side, here are some of the things that need to be done.

1. We need to ensure a very high level of employment in the manufacturing and service fields if agriculture is to stay on its feet in the coming period. This may appear to dodge the problem by focusing attention elsewhere, but the conclusion is inescapable. Farming is by this time inseparably tied up with the rest of the economy, and a depression would hit agriculture doubly hard since it would take away its major market at the same time that the forces we have been describing would come fully into play.

If we do not maintain a reasonably prosperous economy in the future, the only alternative will be a rigidly controlled agriculture in which we try to overcome the effects of technological advance by sharp restrictions on production. For farmers, this will mean close regimentation—and for many, no chance to farm at all. For the rest of us, it will mean needless scarcities of the farm commodities which could be produced.

2. As a corollary to the maintenance of a full domestic market, we must make every effort to work out international trade arrangements which will yield a world outlet. That will mean some competition with our own products, of course, and will eventually lead to regional specialization, but it is essential to the stimulation of world prosperity and to the prevention of agricultural price wars in which no country gains.

The desperate need for food in Europe and Asia offers us at once an opportunity to demonstrate our continuing interest in a peaceful, prosperous world, and a chance to cushion the shock to our economy as the wartime market fades. It would be nothing but good business to help other countries get to their feet during the years ahead.

3. Mechanized farming demands an increased use of agricultural credit. In recent years the Federal government has gone a long way to provide credit to farmers at rates commensurate with those available to urban businessmen. But as we enter the coming era it is highly urgent that we re-examine the adequacy of the credit facilities open to farmers. Before the war the larger operator could generally get along with the

forms of credit provided by private banks, the Federal Land Banks, and the Production Credit Associations. And the very poor farmer was provided a limited supply of credit by the Farm Security Administration through its rehabilitation and tenant-purchase loans.

Falling between these groups, however, there was a considerable number of potentially successful farmers who could not qualify for either type of loan, either because the requirements for FLB and PCA loans were too high, or because those for FSA were too low. Since then the amount of funds available for FSA loans has been stringently curtailed. Thus the often unsatisfactory private loans are the only means of credit available to thousands of farmers who might otherwise make a go of farming.

For the returning veteran the prospect is not much better, since under the GI Bill of Rights the government will guarantee only up to $1000 of a loan for which he himself must find the lender. The Army's poll of servicemen who intended to go into farming revealed that most of them were thinking of investing up to $4000 in a farm, which may be compared with the Department of Agriculture's estimates of $5000 to $8000 as the average cost of a family-sized farm (not counting the necessary tools, equipment, and livestock).

4. In distinguishing between credit and relief needs, it is not intended to rule out the latter. No matter how well our economy functions, there will probably be a need for rural welfare programs just as there will be such needs in urban areas. Nutritional, health, and sanitation requirements on farms are often overlooked simply because they

do not occur in concentrated form. There are slums in the country fully as bad as those in cities, and when we consider our national housing needs we should not neglect the farms.

We do not even have to start at the level of housing construction. It is appalling to contemplate how few rural homes have the most ordinary conveniences of city life. Fewer than one farm home in five had water piped into the house in 1940, and fewer than one in three were lighted by electricity. Moreover, the national averages obscure the fact that these advantages were concentrated in the Hay and Dairy Belt, the Corn Belt, and the valleys of the Far West. Only about 4 per cent of the farm dwellings in four Southern states had piped water, and fewer than 13 per cent had electricity in 1940. Since that time the TVA and local cooperatives sponsored by the Rural Electrification Administration have brought electricity to many additional farms, but the majority of farm housewives still wait for the opportunity to use an electric washing machine and an electric iron.

The possibility of comfortable living for our rural population is here, thanks to the very technology which threatens its disruption. It is important to recognize that the countless human services the farm population lacks can be partly supplied from its own ranks, and thereby provide employment for those who can no longer stay in agricultural production. Rural areas are notoriously deficient in distributional facilities and in medical, educational, and other services, and the life of farming communities will be greatly enriched if their young people have the opportunity to enter these fields.

All of this, it cannot be said too often, depends upon what kind of economy we can achieve under conditions of restored peace. The assurance of a reasonable standard of diet for the American people alone would go a long way toward solving the farm problem. If we can maintain a sufficiently high level of commercial activity to permit agriculture to use its tremendous resources, we shall have done well. If we cannot, we had better look for serious trouble on the farm.

## *"Looking Back at the Crash of 1929"*
**By Floyd Norris**
**From the** New York Times
*October 15, 1999*

*In the late 1990s, talk of the so-called Internet economy was all the rage. Internet technology companies were springing up faster than consumers could click their mice, promising a new economic age of unlimited and perpetual prosperity. Stocks of Internet companies that produced nothing tangible and had never turned a profit were selling for astronomical prices, while Internet millionaires were being made every day.*

*But while these Internet stocks were making investors and brokers on Wall Street rich, their high share prices bore no relation to the actual value of the companies or their products. This situation—the Internet bubble—was very similar to the rampant speculation that preceded the stock market crash of 1929. Sure enough, the Internet bubble burst, and*

*stock prices began to tumble in 2000. Internet technology
stocks, in particular, lost much of their value. As a result
many Internet companies folded, and many individual
American investors lost their savings.*

*In this article, written seventy years after Black
Tuesday,* New York Times *correspondent Floyd Norris revisits the crash of 1929 and draws several disturbing parallels
between it and the American economy of the late 1990s.
Writing about half a year before the Internet bubble began to
burst, Norris's concerns proved insightful and prophetic.*

Seven decades later, the crash of 1929 is remembered as an
unnecessary disaster, a market event that need not have led
to economic collapse. What is not recalled is that people then,
too, were confident about many of the same things that seem
so reassuring today.

"While bubbles that burst are scarcely benign, the consequences need not be catastrophic for the economy," said Alan
Greenspan, the chairman of the Federal Reserve Board, in
congressional testimony this summer. It was not the crash,
but "ensuing failures of policy" that led to the Great
Depression, he said. He seemed confident that he could prevent similar errors if there were another crash, and recalled
how the economy had not been devastated by the 1987 crash.

While considering such self-confidence, it may be useful
to recall an editorial published in *The New York Times* in the
midst of the 1929 crash, on Oct. 26. It heaped scorn on those
who had participated in the "orgy of speculation" that had sent
prices so high amid talk of a new era and permanently high

stock prices. "We shall hear considerably less in the future of those newly invented conceptions of finance which revised the principles of political economy with a view solely to fitting the stock market's vagaries."

But after blasting the speculators, *The Times* took a much more sanguine view of the economy's future. The Federal Reserve had "insured the soundness of the business situation when the speculative markets went on the rocks."

It turned out that such confidence was not well placed. Whether or not the current confidence in the Fed is justified will be known only after a similar crisis arrives, if one does. For now, confidence in Mr. Greenspan has helped to reduce concerns about the possibility of a crash, and thereby probably helped to push stock prices higher.

## *Looking Back at the Crash of '29: Then, as Now, a New Era*

Any look back now at the great stock market boom of the 1920's must inevitably be colored by the boom of the 1990's. Then, as now, leverage helped push prices up. Then anyone could buy stocks by putting up 10 percent of the purchase price. Now, the margin rules call for 50 percent, but that rule is easily evaded by those who wish to do so. Then, as now, there was talk that an exciting new technology had rendered the old economic laws irrelevant. Then, as now, stock connected to that technology zoomed skyward, but even companies that had nothing to do with the technology saw their stock prices benefit.

That technology was radio. Like the Internet, it led to widely publicized new ways to trade stocks. Suddenly, investors and speculators could be closer than ever before to the action. Millions of dollars of stocks were traded from brokerage house offices set up on cruise ships crossing the Atlantic.

Also like the 1990's, the rise in stock prices sparked warnings of excess from skeptics long before the actual top. Alexander D. Noyes, *The Times*' financial editor and probably the most respected financial journalist of the era, wrote a long and persuasive article comparing the 1920's "speculative mania" to previous manias and casting a skeptical eye on the ability of stock prices to continue rising. It was published on Nov. 15, 1925, nearly four years before the crash.

By 1929, such cautionary voices had been discredited, and the stock market had become a force unto itself, propelled by dreams—and the reality—of quick wealth. "Playing the stock market has become a major American pastime," reported *The Times* in a magazine article published on March 24, 1929. The article noted that the number of brokerage accounts had doubled in the past two years, and added, "It is quite true that the people who know the least about the stock market have made the most money out of it in the last few months. Fools who rushed in where wise men feared to tread ran up high gains."

That article was written after the Fed had made its principle stand against stock market speculation, by warning banks not to borrow from the Fed's discount window and then lend the money to stock market speculators. That led to a credit crunch, with interest rates on margin loans rising. The Dow Jones industrial average fell 4 percent the week of March 18–23. Then prices really cracked on Monday March 25 and continued falling until late in the day on Tuesday, when a rally arrived. Before that rally started, the Dow had fallen about 8 percent over less than two days— the equivalent of around 800 points now.

"Responsible bankers agree," *The Times* quoted an unnamed broker as saying that day, after the recovery began, "that stocks should now be supported, having reached a level that makes them attractive."

The responsible banker in question, it turned out, was Charles Mitchell, the president of National City Bank, a predecessor of today's Citibank. He defied the Fed, and lent out all the money the speculators wanted. Soon prices were back on their upward course. By the August peak, the Dow was 35 percent above the low reached during the March sell-off. There was a furor in Washington, but the public and the politicians thought that rising stock prices were good, and the Fed did nothing about Mitchell's defiance.

When the crash arrived in October, it took several days to unfold. The first break came on Thursday, Oct. 24, but there was an afternoon rally that reduced the losses and a decent rise on Friday. But prices were weak on Saturday. (The market traded six days a week in those days.)

Then the floor fell out. On Monday, Oct. 28, the Dow fell 12.8 percent. The next day, thereafter known as Black Tuesday, it lost another 11.7 percent. There would be rallies, but from then on the direction was down. By the time the bottom arrived, in 1932, the Dow was down 89 percent from its 1929 peak.

In rereading *The Times*' coverage of that crash, some things stand out. The paper wanted to cover the news thoroughly and honestly, but it also wanted to be careful not to be alarmist. Each day's headline found something positive to include, such as promises by bankers to aid the market.

Nonetheless, the reporters knew they were witnessing something they had never seen before, as was reflected in two paragraphs below, taken from the lead story on Oct. 30, reporting on Black Tuesday:

"Yesterday's market crash was one which largely affected rich men, institutions, investment trusts and others who participate in the market on a broad and intelligent scale. It was not the margin traders who were caught in the rush to sell, but the rich men of the country who are able to swing blocks of 5,000, 10,000, up to 100,000 shares of high-priced stocks. They went overboard with no more consideration than the little trader who was swept out on the first day of the market's upheaval, whose prices, even at their lowest of last Thursday, now look high by comparison."

"Wall Street was a street of vanished hopes, of curiously silent apprehension and of a sort of paralyzed hypnosis yesterday. Men and women crowded the brokerage offices, even those who have been long since wiped out, and followed the figures on the tape. Little groups gathered here and there to discuss the falling prices in hushed and awed tones. They were participating in the making of financial history. It was the consensus of bankers and brokers alike that no such scenes ever again will be witnessed by this generation. To most of those who have been in the market it is all the more awe-inspiring because their financial history is limited to bull markets."

They were right. Never since has something quite like that been seen. Those who are confident that the Fed will assure that a similar event today would not bring economic disaster might do well to remember that people seventy years ago had faith in the same institution.

## *"'A Soldier Died Today': The Death of FDR, April 12, 1945"*
**By James Agee**
***From* Reporting World War II: American Journalism 1938–1946**
*April 12, 1945*

> Zest for living is one of his most conspicuous charac-
> teristics, and he has enjoyed to the full a job that
> ruined and broke so many other men . . . He rises to an
> emergency as a trout to the fly . . . In Franklin
> Roosevelt there is fireman's blood, and he responds to
> the three-alarm bell like a veteran.
>
> 

—*Marquis W. Childs, "Mr. Roosevelt,"*
Survey Graphic, *May 1, 1940*

*Franklin Roosevelt's death on April 12, 1945, was a shock to the national psyche coming after a decade and a half of his fatherly guidance through an extremely difficult, fright-ening period of enormous national sacrifice, hardship, and trauma, and only four months before the end of World War II. But it is a testament to his energetic leadership that the country, now freed from the crushing burden of the Depression and on the cusp of victory in Europe and the Pacific, would have the strength to confront the unknown and endure whatever was to come.*

*Novelist, poet, screenwriter, journalist, and film critic*
*James Agee had worked for the Works Progress Administration*
*by documenting with photographer Walker Evans the poverty*
*of rural America. In this restrained but deeply moving and*
*evocative piece written upon the death of FDR, Agee records*
*the shock and sadness of a nation that had suddenly lost its*
*father figure and now felt orphaned.*

———□———

In Chungking the spring dawn was milky when an MP on the
graveyard shift picked up the ringing phone in U.S. Army
Headquarters. At first he heard no voice on the other end; then
a San Francisco broadcast coming over the phone line made
clear to him why his informant could find no words. A colonel
came in. The MP just stared at him. The colonel stared back.
After the moment the MP blurted two words. The colonel's jaw
dropped; he hesitated; then without a word he walked away.

It was fresh daylight on Okinawa. Officers and men of
the amphibious fleet were at breakfast when the broadcast
told them. By noon the news was known to the men at the
front, at the far sharp edge of the world's struggle. With no
time for grief, they went on with their work; but there,
while they worked, many a soldier wept.

At home, the news came to people in the hot soft light of
the afternoon, in taxicabs, along the streets, in offices and
bars and factories. In a Cleveland barbershop, 60 year old
Sam Katz was giving a customer a shave when the radio
stabbed out the news. Sam Katz walked over to the water
cooler, took a long, slow drink, sat down and stared into
space for nearly ten minutes. Finally he got up and painted a
sign on his window, "Roosevelt is Dead." Then he finished the

shave. In an Omaha poolhall, men racked up their cues without finishing their games, walked out. In a Manhattan taxicab, a fare told the driver, who pulled over to the curb, sat with his head bowed, and after two minutes resumed his driving.

Everywhere, to almost everyone, the news came with the force of a personal shock. The realization was expressed in the messages of the eminent; it was expressed in the stammering and wordlessness of the humble. A woman in Detroit said: "It doesn't seem possible. It seems to me that he will be back on the radio tomorrow, reassuring us all that it was just a mistake."

It was the same through that evening, and the next day, and the next: the darkened restaurants, the shuttered night-clubs, the hand lettered signs in the windows of stores: "Closed out of Reverence for F.D.R."; the unbroken, 85 hour dirge of the nation's radio; the typical tributes of typical Americans in the death notice columns of their newspapers (said one signed by Samuel and Al Gordon: "A Soldier Died Today")

It was the same on the cotton fields and in the stunned cities between Warm Springs and Washington, while the train, at funeral pace, bore the coffin up April's glowing South in reenactment of Whitman's great threnody.

It was the same in Washington, in the thousands on thousands of grief wrung faces which walled the caisson's grim progression with prayers and with tears. It was the same on Sunday morning in the gentle landscape at Hyde Park, when the burial service of the Episcopal Church spoke its old, strong, quiet words of farewell; and it was the same at that later moment when all save the gravemen were withdrawn and reporters, in awe felt hiding, saw how a brave woman, a widow, returned, and watched over the grave alone, until the grave was filled.

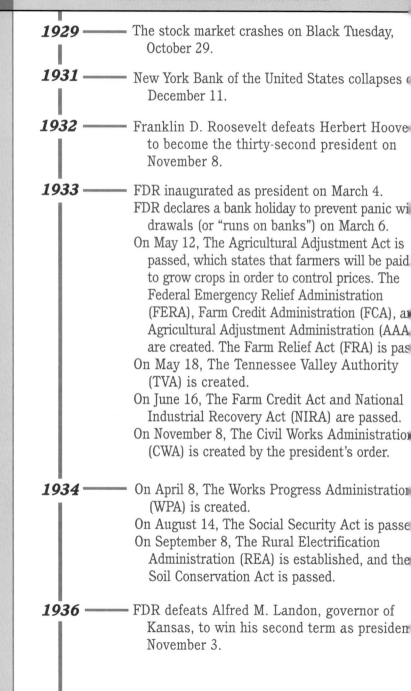

# TIMELINE

**1929** — The stock market crashes on Black Tuesday, October 29.

**1931** — New York Bank of the United States collapses on December 11.

**1932** — Franklin D. Roosevelt defeats Herbert Hoover to become the thirty-second president on November 8.

**1933** — FDR inaugurated as president on March 4.
FDR declares a bank holiday to prevent panic withdrawals (or "runs on banks") on March 6.
On May 12, The Agricultural Adjustment Act is passed, which states that farmers will be paid to grow crops in order to control prices. The Federal Emergency Relief Administration (FERA), Farm Credit Administration (FCA), and Agricultural Adjustment Administration (AAA) are created. The Farm Relief Act (FRA) is passed.
On May 18, The Tennessee Valley Authority (TVA) is created.
On June 16, The Farm Credit Act and National Industrial Recovery Act (NIRA) are passed.
On November 8, The Civil Works Administration (CWA) is created by the president's order.

**1934** — On April 8, The Works Progress Administration (WPA) is created.
On August 14, The Social Security Act is passed.
On September 8, The Rural Electrification Administration (REA) is established, and the Soil Conservation Act is passed.

**1936** — FDR defeats Alfred M. Landon, governor of Kansas, to win his second term as president November 3.

**1937** — In May, the economic recovery stops, and the economy enters a second depression.

On July 22, The Farm Security Agency (FSA) is created, establishing camps and medical care and helping migrant farm workers find jobs.

On September 1, The U.S. Housing Authority (USHA) is created to provide slum clearance, construction projects, and rent subsidies.

**1938** — On June 25, The Fair Labor Standards Act is passed, enacting the first national minimum wage law.

**1940** — FDR defeats Wendell Willkie to win his third term as president on November 5.

**1941** — The Japanese attack Pearl Harbor, Hawaii, on December 7.

On December 8, the United States declares war on Japan.

On December 11, Germany and Italy declare war on the United States.

**1944** — America and her allies invade the European continent on D-day, April 12.

On November 7, FDR defeats Thomas E. Dewey to win his fourth term as president.

**1945** — On April 12, FDR dies at Warm Springs, Georgia, and Vice President Harry S. Truman is sworn in as the thirty-third president.

On May 7, Germany surrenders unconditionally to the Allied forces.

On August 6, an atomic bomb is dropped on Hiroshima, Japan.

On August 9, an atomic bomb is dropped on Nagasaki, Japan.

On September 2, Japan surrenders, ending World War II.

# FOR MORE INFORMATION

## Web Sites

Due to the changing nature of Internet links, the Rosen
Publishing Group, Inc., has developed an online list of
Web sites related to the subject of this book. This site is
updated regularly. Please use this link to access the list:

http://www.rosenlinks.com/canf/depr

# FOR FURTHER READING

Cohen, Robert, ed. *Dear Mrs. Roosevelt: Letters from Children of
the Great Depression*. Chapel Hill, NC: University of North
Carolina Press, 2002.

Grant, R. G. *The Great Depression*. New York: Barrons
Educational Series, 2003.

Meltzer, Milton. *Brother, Can You Spare a Dime? The Great Depression 1929–1933*. New York: New American Library, 1991.

Moss, Marissa. *Rose's Journal: The Story of a Girl in the Great
Depression*. New York: Harcourt, 2001.

Stein, R. Conrad. *The Great Depression.* New York: Children's
Book Press, 1993.

Steinbeck, John. *The Grapes of Wrath.* New York: Penguin, 1992.

Uys, Errol Lincoln. *Riding the Rails: Teenagers on the Move
During the Great Depression.* New York: Routledge, 2003.

Worster, Donald. *Dust Bowl: The Southern Plains in the 1930s.*
New York: Oxford University Press, 1982.

Abrams, Charles. "Housing and Politics." _Survey Graphic_, Vol. 29, No. 2, February 1, 1940, p. 91.

Charles Abrams, an author who specialized in housing issues, examines the controversy, passion, and politics surrounding the government's first attempts to build public and subsidized housing.

Agee, James. "'A Soldier Died Today': The Death of FDR, April 12, 1945." In _Reporting World War II: American Journalism 1938–1946_, edited by Samuel Hynes, Anne Matthews, and Nancy Caldwell. New York: Library of America, 2001.

In this piece, written upon the death of FDR, James Agee eulogizes the president who saved Americans from hunger and despair.

Anonymous. "Caught in the Trough." _The Atlantic Monthly_, June 1932, pp. 658–662.

This anonymous first-person account of a middle-class family's valiant struggle to stave off poverty reveals the true extent of the Depression and the suffering it unleashed.

Dell'Orto, Giovanna. "Keeping an Eye on America: The Contradictions of Depression-Era Photography." Review of _The Documentary Eye: Depression-Era Photography_ from the Weisman Art Museum Collection. _Minnesota Daily_, February 13, 1998.

This is a review of a 1998 art exhibit of Depression-era photography at the Weisman Art Museum in Minneapolis, Minnesota, written by Giovanna Dell'Orto, a journalist for the _Minnesota Daily_.

Epstein, Abraham. "'Social Security' Under the New Deal."
*The Nation*, September 15, 1935, p. 261. Reprinted with
permission from the September 4, 1935, issue of the
*Nation*. For subscription information, call 1-800-333-8526.
Portions of each week's *The Nation* magazine can be
accessed at http://www.thenation.com.
Abraham Epstein, a leading advocate for old-age security,
describes the chaotic, controversial, and hurried birth of
Social Security in this 1935 article from the *Nation*.

Hickok, Lorena. Letter to Harry L. Hopkins regarding the
Tennessee Valley Authority (TVA). June 6, 1934.
From 1933 to 1936, Lorena Hickok, former Associated
Press reporter and close friend of Eleanor Roosevelt, wrote
field reports for FDR advisor Harry Hopkins and the Federal
Emergency Relief Agency. The letter to Hopkins reprinted
here is Hickok's exuberant account of the transformation of
the Tennessee Valley under the Tennessee Valley Authority.

Hutchison, Keith. "Starving on Relief." *The Nation*, February 12,
1936, p. 186. Reprinted with permission from the February
12, 1936, issue of *The Nation*. For subscription information,
call 1-800-333-8526. Portions of each week's *The Nation*
magazine can be accessed at http://www.thenation.com.
In this selection, Keith Hutchison, a regular contributor
to *The Nation* during the Depression who often examined
the progress of the New Deal, offers a raw exposé of the
tragic shortcomings of FDR's relief program.

Le Sueur, Meridel. "Cows and Horses Are Hungry." *American
Mercury*, September 1934.
Meridel Le Sueur, a reporter and children's book author,

offers a surreal and disturbing description of the drought
and Dust Bowl conditions plaguing the Great Plains.

McCausland, Elizabeth. "Save the Arts Projects." *The Nation*, July
17, 1937, pp. 67–69. Reprinted with permission from the
July 17, 1937, issue of the *Nation*. For subscription information, call 1-800-333-8526. Portions of each week's *The Nation*
magazine can be accessed at http://www.thenation.com.
Elizabeth McCausland, an art critic for several Depression-
era arts magazines, provides a spirited defense of the
Federal Art Project and its contributions to the rebuilding of
a shattered America and a plea for its continued funding.

McGovern, James R. "Americans Go to the Movies." *And a
Time for Hope: Americans in the Great Depression*. Westport,
CT: Praeger, 2001.
In *And a Time for Hope: Americans in the Great Depression*,
James R. McGovern, Emeritus Professor of History at the
University of West Florida, presents a social history of the
United States in the 1930s.

Norris, Floyd. "Looking Back at the Crash of 1929." *New
York Times*, October 15, 1999. Copyright ©1999 The
New York Times Co. Reprinted with permission.
In this article, written seventy years after Black Tuesday,
*New York Times* correspondent Floyd Norris revisits the
crash of 1929 and draws several disturbing parallels
between it and the American economy of the late 1990s.
Writing about a half year before the Internet bubble began
to burst, Norris's concerns proved insightful and prophetic.

Penny, Lucrecia. "Pea-Pickers' Child Dies." *Survey Graphic*,
Vol. 24, No. 7, July 1935, p. 352.

Lucrecia Penny offers a stark account of the death of the child of migrant workers. The author exposes the desperate living conditions experienced by many of the nation's impoverished agricultural workers.

Procter, Walter G. Letter to Franklin D. Roosevelt. FDR Library. October 10, 1935.

This is one of the letters solicited by FDR in which clergymen reported on the material state of their parishioners.

Roosevelt, Eleanor. "What We Are Fighting For." *American Magazine*, July 1942, pp. 16–17, 60–62.

In this magazine piece, Eleanor Roosevelt offers the moral rationale for American involvement in World War II, an argument very much rooted in economics, social justice, and the lingering effects of the Depression.

Roosevelt, Franklin D. "Outlining the New Deal program" (Fireside chat). Washington, D.C., May 7, 1933.

The fireside chat reproduced here served as America's introduction to FDR's proposed New Deal program—a collection of policies and projects designed to pull the nation out of the Great Depression.

Steinbeck, John. "The Harvest Gypsies." *San Francisco News*, October 5 and 12, 1936.

John Steinbeck's reporting on California's migrant labor camps for the *San Francisco News* provided the genesis for his later celebrated novel *The Grapes of Wrath* (1939). In this two-part series, Steinbeck offers an unflinching but sympathetic look at the grim conditions and sense of despair experienced by America's impoverished agricultural laborers.

"Stocks Collapse in 16,410,030-Share Day, but Rally at Close Cheers Brokers; Bankers Optimistic, to Continue Aid." *New*

*York Times*, October 30, 1929. Copyright © 1929 The New York Times Co. Reprinted with permission.

This article was written on October 29, 1929—Black Tuesday—and ran in the *New York Times* the following day. It reports the grim details of the worst stock market crash in history as it was happening. Because of the immediacy of the events and the reporting, notes of optimism are sounded in ignorance of the decadelong depression that lay ahead.

Street, James H. "The Tractor Revolution." *The Atlantic Monthly*, June 1946, pp. 111–115.

James H. Street, an agricultural economist with the Department of Agriculture, sounds a few warning notes in this *Atlantic Monthly* article about the dangers posed to American farmers and the economy by agricultural mechanization. Looking back at the 1930s in order to look forward and avoid similar ecological and economic catastrophes, Street proposes a program for the health and viability of post-Depression American agriculture.

Todd, Charles L. "Trampling Out the Vintage." *Common Sense*, July 1939, pp. 7–8, 30.

Charles L. Todd, an ethnographer and folk musicologist, documented the work of the Farm Security Administration in California. In this article for *Common Sense*, he reports on the setting up of safe work camps for "Okie" migrant workers.

Woodward, Ellen. "The Lasting Values of the WPA." WPA papers. 1935.

In this speech, Ellen Woodward, director of the WPA's Women's and Professional Division, argues for the practical and historic importance of the WPA.

# INDEX

## About the Editor

Paul Kupperberg is a freelance writer and an editor for DC Comics. He has published more than 700 comic books, stories, articles, and books, as well as several years' worth of the *Superman* and *Tom & Jerry* newspaper comic strips. *Critical Perspectives on the Great Depression* is his fourth book for Rosen. Paul lives in Connecticut with his wife, Robin, and son, Max.

## Credits

Cover, p.1 © Corbis.

Designer: Thomas Forget; Series Editor: John Kemmerer